VISUAL QUICKSTART GUIDE

WORDPRESS

Jessica Neuman Beck and Matt Beck

 Peachpit Press

Visual QuickStart Guide

WordPress

Jessica Neuman Beck and Matt Beck

Peachpit Press

1249 Eighth Street
Berkeley, CA 94710
510/524-2178
510/524-2221 (fax)

Find us on the Web at www.peachpit.com
To report errors, please send a note to errata@peachpit.com
Peachpit Press is a division of Pearson Education

Copyright © 2010 by Jessica Neuman Beck and Matthew Beck
Acquisitions Editor: Wendy Sharp
Project Editor: Valerie Witte
Production Editor: Danielle Foster
Developmental Editors: Becky Morgan and Valerie Witte
Technical Editor: Aaron Hockley
Copyeditor: Liz Welch
Proofreader: Patricia Pane
Composition: Danielle Foster
Indexer: James Minkin

ISBN-13: 978-0-321-67921-5
ISBN–10:   0-321-67921-0

9 8 7 6 5 4 3 2 1

Printed and bound in the United States of America

Acknowledgments

Jessica and Matt would like to thank the editorial staff at Peachpit and the Portland WordPress community, without which this book would not have been possible.

Thanks, guys!

CONTENTS AT A GLANCE

TABLE OF CONTENTS

TABLE OF CONTENTS

TABLE OF CONTENTS

INTRODUCTION

WordPress is an open source blogging platform with the largest user base of any self-hosted blogging tool. Users can set up a blog on WordPress.com or install WordPress with a hosting company or on a personal server, allowing for flexibility and easy customization. It's highly extensible, with a veritable treasure trove of add-ons and plug-ins available both on the official WordPress.org site and elsewhere on the Internet. Since the project is open source, it's easy for developers to work with—and it's free!

In this introduction, we talk about what a blog is and how to use it. We'll tell you a little more about WordPress and give you an overview of the new features in WordPress 2.8. We'll also explore the differences between WordPress.org and WordPress.com to help you decide which one is right for you.

In this book we'll be focusing primarily on WordPress.org, the self-hosted version of WordPress, which offers the most flexibility and customization options, but WordPress.com is a solid choice for many users who don't require a lot from their blogging engine.

Blogs Explained

A blog is a Web site that displays posts or articles in sequential order, with the newest posts appearing first. The word *blog* comes from *Weblog*, itself a contraction of *Web* and *log*.

Blogs began as online journals, usually featuring a single author writing about a specific topic or interest. However, blogs have expanded to encompass news sites, magazine-style sites, and even corporate Web sites, in addition to personal journals.

Blogs often fill a niche, focusing on a particular subject, and often encourage reader participation by enabling comments on articles or posts.

According to Technorati (technorati.com/blogging/state-of-the-blogosphere/), there have been over 133 million blog records indexed since 2002, making the blog the most popular type of site on the Internet.

The blog format tends toward the following:

◆ A new page is automatically generated for each post.

◆ Each post is defined by one or more categories.

◆ Posts can be further categorized by tags.

◆ Posts can be read sequentially or browsed in archives by date, category, or tag.

◆ Design and layout are dictated by a predefined template or theme; changes to the theme affect the look and feel of the site but do not affect content (making it easy to modify a site's look).

Anatomy of a WordPress Blog

While blogs can vary widely in layout, most contain these six basic segments. We're using the default WordPress theme as an example of a typical blog layout.

◆ **Header:** This section usually includes the blog's name and a graphic (**Figure I.1**).

◆ **Tagline (optional):** The tagline or slogan often gives the reader a better idea of what the blog is about. The WordPress default is "Just another WordPress weblog."

◆ **Navigation:** This consists of internal links to the different sections of the site, such as Archives, Contact, About, and Home.

continues on next page

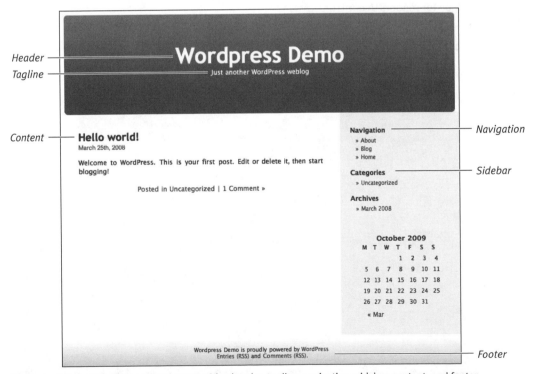

Figure i.1 A typical WordPress blog layout, with a header, tagline, navigation, sidebar, content, and footer.

◆ **Content:** This section changes depending on what section of the blog is being viewed; for example, on the home page the content may be an overview of the latest posts, while the contact page would include information and perhaps a form for getting in touch with the blog's author.

◆ **Sidebar:** Additional navigation may be located here as well as snippets of code known as *widgets*, which may contain information such as the author's latest Twitter posts, polls, an overview of recent comments, or photos recently posted to Flickr.

◆ **Footer:** This section usually contains copyright and design information.

In addition, each post's page contains information specific to the post, such as the time and date of posting, the author(s), the categories and/or tags, and (if comments are enabled) a place for readers to contribute their thoughts.

What's New in WordPress 2.8

WordPress 2.8 is the latest version of the popular open source blogging platform that powers hundreds of thousands of blogs all around the world. Released in June 2009, WordPress 2.8 was downloaded over 1.5 million times in the first three months and continues to be a popular choice for bloggers and site owners.

WordPress 2.8 debuted some major improvements to the look and feel of the WordPress back end, making the administration section easier and more intuitive. With the release of WordPress 2.8, users are better able to quickly install, manage, and style a site. Here are some of the most significant changes:

◆ A new drag-and-drop admin interface for widget management

◆ Built-in syntax highlighting and function lookup in plug-in and theme editors

◆ Ability to browse the theme directory and install themes from the admin screen

◆ Enhanced customization options for the Dashboard

◆ Support for time zones and automatic daylight saving time adjustment

◆ Faster loading of admin pages

INTRODUCTION

WordPress.org vs. WordPress.com

There are three different versions of WordPress: WordPress.org, WordPress.com, and WordPress MU. WordPress.org is the most common; it's a self-installed version that resides on your own Web server (most likely on a hosting account). WordPress.com is a free blog hosted by WordPress (meaning you can use it without a separate hosting account). WordPress MU (Multi-User) is similar to WordPress.org, but allows the user to create and manage many different blogs from one installation. We won't be covering WordPress MU here, but if you are interested in learning more about the multiuser version, you can find lots of great information at http://mu.wordpress.org.

Here's a handy reference table so you can quickly see the difference between WordPress.org and WordPress.com (**Table I.1**).

Ultimately, the version you decide to use will depend on your specific needs. Both WordPress.com and WordPress.org are excellent products that serve up the same core function: blogging.

So how do you know which version of WordPress is right for you?

At first glance, a blog hosted on WordPress.com is similar to the self-hosted version. Like other hosted blogging services such as TypePad and Blogger, WordPress.com allows basic theme customization (from a preapproved set of themes) and lets users add pages, sidebars, and widgets. The free account takes only seconds to set up. Free users are given a subdomain at [yourname].wordpress.com and currently get 3 GB of storage for images and media. Options like theme styling, suppression of WordPress text ads, and a custom domain name are available for a fee. It's a good solution for beginners looking to have an online presence without owning a domain name or paying for Web hosting.

Table I.1

Comparison of WordPress.org and WordPress.com

WORDPRESS.ORG

- Free to use
- Installed on your own Web server or Web-hosting account
- Ads are not included by default (though bloggers may choose to run their own ads)
- Hundreds of plug-ins and themes
- Fully customizable
- Analytic statistics as a plug-in or add-on
- Unlimited user accounts
- Requires setup
- Free to use existing domain

WORDPRESS.COM

- Free to use basic version
- Hosted on wordpress.com
- Ads are displayed on your blog
- Limited selection of plug-ins and themes
- Features can be extended by paying for premium services
- Built-in analytic statistics
- Number of users is limited
- Easiest to set up
- Using your own domain name is a premium service

However, if you're an advanced user, a Web professional, or someone using WordPress for business, you need to be able to modify and customize your site to create a unique brand experience. That's where the self-hosted version of WordPress from WordPress.org comes in. With it, you have full control over every aspect of your site. You'll be able to build your own theme, install plug-ins, and easily modify your design. This is particularly important if you want to use WordPress as a lightweight content management system (commonly referred to as a CMS), rather than "just a blog." With a self-hosted WordPress installation, you can create a full-featured site that functions in whatever way you want it to, limited only by your imagination (and your knowledge of theme building). Your visitors don't even need know that you're running WordPress!

✔ Tips

- If you already have a Web-hosting account, odds are your hosting company supports WordPress. Most of them do, and many offer easy installers to make setup easier for you.

- WordPress runs on PHP and MySQL, but you can easily get running with only minimal knowledge of each.

- A breakdown of the requirements for running the latest version of WordPress is available at www.wordpress.org/about/requirements.

FIRST STEPS

This chapter will walk you through the process of getting started with WordPress. Not sure whether to choose a hosting account or your own server? Not sure how to install WordPress?

We'll break down the pros and cons of using a hosting account versus hosting WordPress on your own server, and we'll give you some tips on choosing a compatible Web host to make your WordPress installation as easy as possible.

We'll give you step-by-step instructions for installing WordPress using Fantastico and other installers; creating a MySQL database both in a hosting control panel and phpMyAdmin; and using the WordPress installer.

You're just steps away from your first WordPress blog!

Setting Up WordPress

There are several ways to set up WordPress, and many of them depend on the type of hosting you use. Most hosting companies now offer WordPress installers or installation assistance, so if you have an existing hosting account it's worthwhile to see if your host is one of them.

If your hosting account uses the very popular cPanel control panel, odds are you have access to the Fantastico De Luxe autoinstaller, which allows you to easily install many different applications—including WordPress. For more information on Fantastico, go to www.netenberg.com/fantastico.php.

If you don't have Fantastico, don't worry; we will walk you through a manual setup process in which you first create a database and then run the WordPress installer.

A Hosting Account or Your Own Server?

Unless you anticipate high traffic or have a specific need, it probably isn't worth the trouble to set up your own Web server. Most hosting companies now support WordPress sites, and hosting is generally cheaper to buy than it is to maintain yourself. However, if you already have your own Web server you can easily configure it to allow you to run WordPress.

Meeting the minimum requirements for WordPress to run on your server is simple. You can find a comprehensive rundown at http://wordpress.org/about/requirements. The major required applications are PHP version 4.3 or higher and MySQL version 4.0 or higher.

WordPress will run on Windows servers and Internet Information Services (IIS), but Linux and Apache are recommended for the Apache mod_rewrite module's ability to create friendly URLs.

Figure 1.1 Begin by logging in with your administrative user account and password.

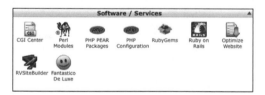

Figure 1.2 The cPanel menu lets you control many aspects of your hosting account.

Figure 1.3 The Fantastico autoinstaller is an easy way to set up WordPress.

Using an Installer

One of the nice things about installing WordPress is that many hosting companies provide an autoinstaller that takes care of creating the required database, creating all the files and directories that WordPress needs to run as well as setting basic configuration options. These installers are excellent tools for this task and really do make things easy for you.

If you aren't sure what your hosting company offers, ask them. It's likely that they offer an installer of some sort, or at least assistance in the installation process.

To install WordPress using Fantastico:

1. In your browser, navigate to the URL of your cPanel (control panel) and log in using your administrative user account and password (**Figure 1.1**).

2. Once you are logged in, locate and select the smiley face icon labeled Fantastico De Luxe.

   The arrangement of your cPanel windows varies from hosting company to hosting company, but this icon is most likely to be located under Software/Services (**Figure 1.2**).

3. In the left panel under Blogs, click WordPress to start the installation process (**Figure 1.3**).

continues on next page

4. The first WordPress installer screen shows requirements and previously installed copies of WordPress for your hosting account (if any). To create a new WordPress installation, click the New Installation link (**Figure 1.4**).

5. Fill out the fields under Install WordPress 1/3, paying careful attention to the onscreen instructions (**Figure 1.5**).

Here's where you will set a username and password for your WordPress admin account and provide general details about your blog. The site name and description you enter here will be displayed on your Web site and can be changed later—but your administrative username and password can't, so choose carefully! When you have completed all the fields, click the Install WordPress button to continue.

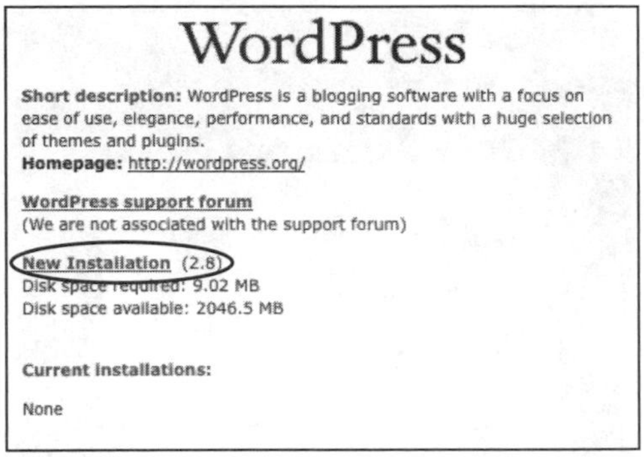

Figure 1.4 Click the New Installation link.

Figure 1.5 Fantastico WordPress installer 1/3 (screen 1 of 3).

Choosing a Hosting Company

WordPress hosting is easy to find, but how do you know if you're setting up with a good company or one with lots of problems?

In this instance, a little bit of research can go a long way. Switching from one hosting company to another can be a complicated process, especially when you need to transfer data-intensive applications like WordPress. You can find a short list of recommended hosts online at http://wordpress.org/hosting/.

If none of those look good to you, check for recommendations. An Internet search can often provide links to reviews of a specific company, and you can always ask other bloggers what hosting company they use and if they'd recommend the service.

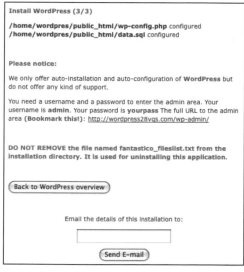

Install WordPress (2/3)

The MySQL database and MySQL user **wordpres_wrdp1** will be created and used for this installation.

- You chose to install in the main directory of the domain **wordpress28vqs.com**.
- The access URL will be: **http://wordpress28vqs.com/**.

Click on **Finish Installation** to continue.

(Finish installation)

Figure 1.6 Fantastico WordPress installer 2/3 (screen 2 of 3).

Install WordPress (3/3)

/home/wordpres/public_html/wp-config.php configured
/home/wordpres/public_html/data.sql configured

Please notice:

We only offer auto-installation and auto-configuration of **WordPress** but do not offer any kind of support.

You need a username and a password to enter the admin area. Your username is **admin**. Your password is **yourpass** The full URL to the admin area (**Bookmark this!**): http://wordpress28vqs.com/wp-admin/

DO NOT REMOVE the file named fantastico_fileslist.txt from the installation directory. It is used for uninstalling this application.

(Back to WordPress overview)

Email the details of this installation to:

[   ]
(Send E-mail)

Figure 1.7 Fantastico WordPress installer 3/3 (screen 3 of 3).

6. The next screen gives you information about the installation that Fantastico is going to create for you. Look this information over carefully. If everything looks correct, click Finish Installation (**Figure 1.6**).

That's it! WordPress is now installed. The final installer screen recaps the settings you selected when you installed it and provides a URL to your WordPress installation (**Figure 1.7**).

✔ Tips

■ If you aren't sure whether your hosting account uses cPanel and Fantastico, this information is usually included in the welcome e-mail you received from the hosting company when you signed up for your account.

■ Fantastico can be used to install many more applications than just WordPress. Your available options will vary depending on your hosting company, but common options include shopping cart software, other blogging platforms, forums, and more.

Installing WordPress Using Other Installers

Our example uses the Fantastico De Luxe installer via cPanel, a common hosting control panel. However, many hosting companies use other control panels and installers. Some hosts have even built their own installers, which can further simplify the process.

If your hosting company doesn't use cPanel on its servers, contact your hosting company's support staff or search through their online support pages for WordPress. It's a good bet that installation instructions already exist.

Setting Up a Database

WordPress requires a MySQL database to store the information for your site, such as your blog posts, page content, usernames and passwords, settings, and more.

If you use an installer like Fantastico to set up WordPress, this database will be automatically created for you. If not, you will need to set one up yourself.

To set up a MySQL database using a hosting control panel:

1. In your browser, navigate to the URL of your cPanel (control panel) and log in using your administrative user account and password.

2. In the Databases section, select MySQL Database Wizard (**Figure 1.8**).

3. The first screen of the database wizard simply asks you to name the database you wish to create, and provides a button that will display an instructional video. Type the name of your database in the New Database field (wordpress in our example), and click Next Step to continue (**Figure 1.9**).

   Although you can use any unique name for your database, using a simple descriptive name will make things easier for you if you later need to install additional databases for other applications.

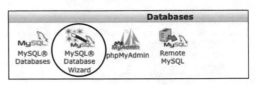

Figure 1.8 Under Databases, click MySQL Database Wizard.

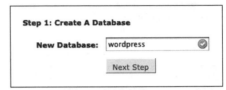

Figure 1.9 Step 1 of the MySQL Database Wizard is creating a database.

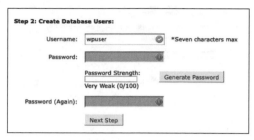

Figure 1.10 Step 2 of the MySQL Database Wizard is creating database users.

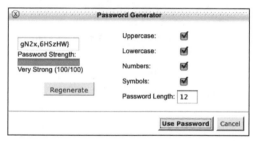

Figure 1.11 The MySQL Database Wizard generates a password for you.

4. In step 2 of the Database Wizard, you will need to create a MySQL username and password that will allow WordPress to store and retrieve all the information it needs to function. Enter a username (wpuser in our example) and click Generate Password (**Figure 1.10**).

5. In the pop-up window that appears, you will see that cPanel has automatically created a password that will be difficult for anyone to guess. This is a good security measure, and it's the recommended method of setting this password (**Figure 1.11**). Click Use Password to populate the password fields on this screen and again click Next Step to continue to the next screen.

You can create a password manually, but the random password is usually a better choice. You won't need to type this password to log in to WordPress or anything else; it's only needed during setup, so don't worry about it being hard to remember.

continues on next page

6. At the top of the screen you will now see the actual username and password that were created (**Figure 1.12**). Note in our example that the *wordpres_* prefix has been added to the wpuser username we typed in. Make a note of the username and password for use when you install WordPress later. This screen also asks you what permissions you want to give the MySQL user for the database you are creating. Click All Privileges to check all the boxes, and then click Next Step to continue.

A confirmation screen will appear telling you that the user has been added to the database (**Figure 1.13**). Your MySQL database has been created and a user account has been added to it for WordPress to use. You can now move on to "Installing WordPress."

✔ Tip

■ In step 4 you saw "Added database *name-of-database*" at the top of the screen; note that in our example, the database that was created is actually *wordpres_wordpress*, not *wordpress* as we typed it back in Figure 1.11. This is because cPanel hosting accounts are almost always used in a shared server setup, so many other people also have accounts on the same Web server. The *wordpres_* prefix keeps our database information separate from other users on the system. Make note of the actual database name for use when you install WordPress later.

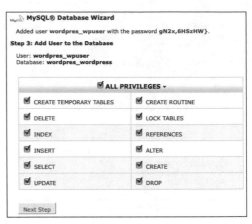

Figure 1.12 Step 3 of the MySQL Database Wizard is adding the user to the database.

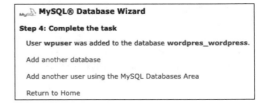

Figure 1.13 Step 4 of the MySQL Database Wizard is completing the task.

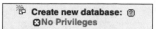

Figure 1.14 If you see No Privileges, this means you won't be able to use this method of setting up the MySQL database.

Locate the Create New Database section to start the process

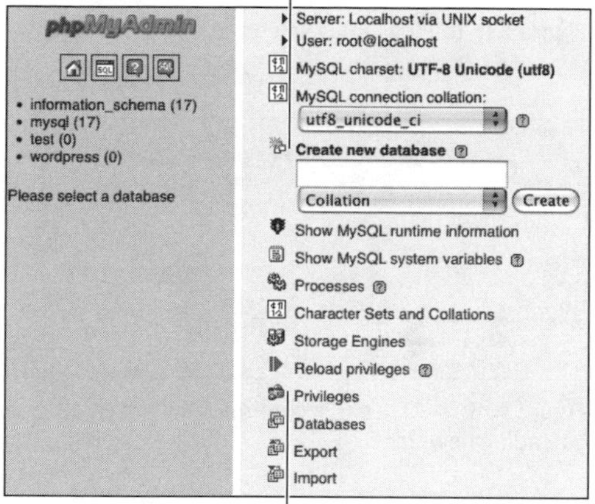

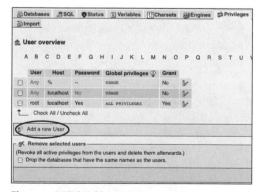

Click here to set up MySQL Database

Figure 1.15 You'll use this menu to create your database.

To set up a MySQL Database using phpMyAdmin:

1. Sign in to phpMyAdmin on your hosting account. The URL you'll need to use for this task varies from host to host.

2. Look for the section Create New Database. If you see a red X and the words No Privileges, you won't be able to use this method of setting up the MySQL database (**Figure 1.14**).

   This is fairly common on shared server hosting, such as cPanel. Don't worry: you can still use phpMyAdmin to administer databases, but you'll have to create the database using the tools provided by your hosting company. However, if you see a blank text box below Create New Database, click Privileges to set up your database (**Figure 1.15**).

3. Once you've displayed the Privileges screen of the database administration screen, click Add A New User to continue (**Figure 1.16**).

   continues on next page

Figure 1.16 Click Add A New User.

4. Enter a username (wordpress in our example) and a password. Click Generate, and then Copy to let the system generate a strong password for you automatically (**Figure 1.17**). You could manually enter a password here, but we don't recommend it.

5. Make a note of the username and password so you'll have them when you install WordPress; then make sure that Create Database With Same Name And Grant All Privileges is selected under Database For User and click Go.

You should see a confirmation screen telling you that you have added a new user (**Figure 1.18**). If you do, that means the database was created correctly and you can now move on to the next section.

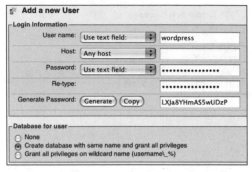

Figure 1.17 You'll use this screen to add a new user.

Figure 1.18 You'll see this confirmation screen after you add a new user.

Using Other MySQL Installers

It's beyond the scope of this book to list and explain every method of creating the database and user account needed to set up WordPress, so we've provided examples using two popular installation methods: cPanel and phpMyAdmin.

Many hosting companies use other control panels that will allow you to set up the required database and user account in a similar fashion. If you're not sure how to set up MySQL for your WordPress site, we recommend contacting your hosting company's support staff or looking at their online documentation. Many companies provide online tutorials in a knowledge base on their Web site that will help walk you through the process.

Installing WordPress

WordPress boasts the "famous 5-minute installation process," which means you'll be up and blogging in no time. Follow these easy steps to install WordPress on your server.

To run the WordPress installer:

1. In your browser, go to www.wordpress.org/download/ and click the Download button (**Figure 1.19**).

continues on next page

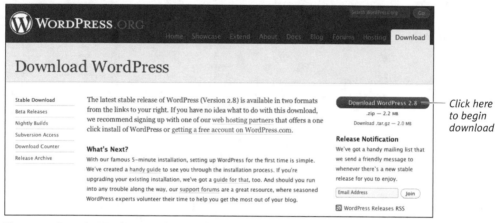

Figure 1.19 Go to the WordPress Web site and click Download.

2. Download and extract the ZIP file containing the WordPress installation files.

3. Open your favorite FTP client and enter the settings provided to you by your hosting company and sign in.

4. You should see a list of files and directories on your Web server as well as on your local computer (**Figure 1.20**). Navigate to the directory where you wish to install WordPress on the server.

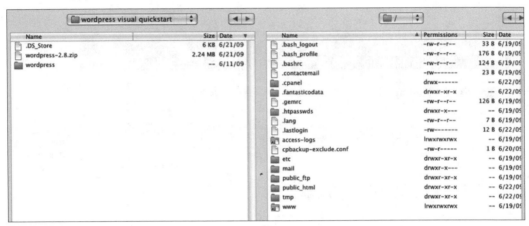

Figure 1.20 In your FTP client, navigate to the directory where you want to install WordPress.

5. Find the extracted files from the ZIP file you downloaded in step 2; select them and drag them into the installation directory on the server to upload the files (**Figure 1.21**). Depending on your Internet connection, this process may take several minutes to complete.

continues on next page

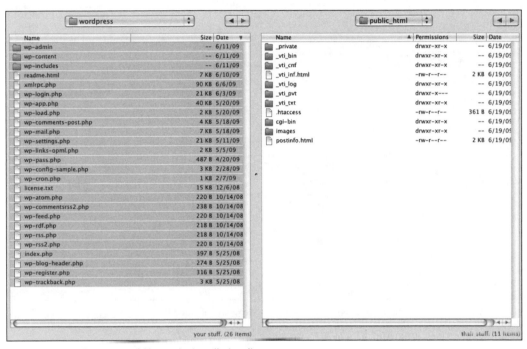

Figure 1.21 Drag the extracted files to the installation directory.

6. When an upload is complete, most FTP client software will alert you with a sound or a pop-up window. Take a quick look at the list of files on the server to make sure everything you uploaded is there (**Figure 1.22**).

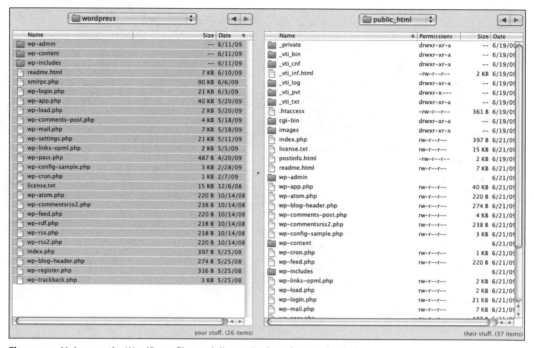

Figure 1.22 Make sure the WordPress files and directories have been uploaded.

There doesn't seem to be a wp-config.php file. I need this before we can get started. Need more help? We got it. You can create a wp-config.php file through a web interface, but this doesn't work for all server setups. The safest way is to manually create the file.

Create a Configuration File

Figure 1.23 Click the Create A Configuration File button.

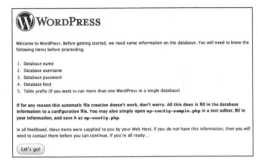

WORDPRESS

Welcome to WordPress. Before getting started, we need some information on the database. You will need to know the following items before proceeding.

1. Database name
2. Database username
3. Database password
4. Database host
5. Table prefix (if you want to run more than one WordPress in a single database)

If for any reason this automatic file creation doesn't work, don't worry. All this does is fill in the database information into a configuration file. You may also simply open wp-config-sample.php in a text editor, fill in your information, and save it as wp-config.php.

In all likelihood, these items were supplied to you by your Web Host. If you do not have this information, then you will need to contact them before you can continue. If you're all ready...

Let's go!

Figure 1.24 Click the Let's Go! button to continue.

7. In your browser, navigate to the URL of your new site (this will be your main URL if you installed WordPress in the main directory, or a URL with a slash and a folder name if you installed it in a sub-directory). You should see the first screen of the WordPress installer (**Figure 1.23**). Click Create A Configuration File to continue. If you get an error that says, "Sorry, I can't write to the directory" at this stage, it will be due to file system permissions on the server. If this happens, proceed to step 8; otherwise skip to step 10.

8. Find the file wp-config-sample in the downloaded and extracted directory and rename the file **wp-config.php**. Open the file in a text editor such as Notepad, BBEdit, or TextMate, and enter the database settings as described in the file under the comment `// ** MySQL settings - You can get this info from your web host ** //` (you'll need the MySQL username and password, as well as the database name). Once that's done, use your FTP client to upload the file to the server.

9. Reload your new site in your browser to continue. (Since steps 10 and 11 deal with an alternate method of creating the wp-config.php file, you can skip them and go to step 12).

10. If your server's permission settings will allow you to automatically create the wp-config.php file, you'll be looking at the Welcome To WordPress page. Click Let's Go! to continue (**Figure 1.24**).

continues on next page

11. Enter all your database connection details: you'll need to know the name of the database as well as the MySQL username and password you created earlier (**Figure 1.25**). The odds are high that the database host will stay set to localhost. If you intend to install only one blog, the default setting of wp_ is fine. If you intend to run multiple copies of WordPress out of the same database, you'll also need to change the table prefix to something unique. Once you finish, click Submit.

12. You should see a confirmation page telling you that the first part of the installation is complete. Click Run The Install to continue (**Figure 1.26**).

13. Under Information Needed, enter the title of your blog and your e-mail address (**Figure 1.27**). (You can also select whether you wish your site to be indexed by search engines.) The title you enter here will almost always be displayed on your site; you can change it later. Be sure that you've entered a valid e-mail address for yourself and click Install WordPress.

14. On the Success screen (**Figure 1.28**), take careful note of the automatically generated password for the admin account. You'll need this password the first time you log in. Click Log In to continue.

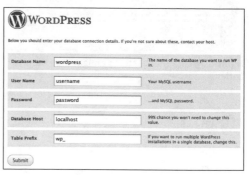

Figure 1.25 Complete these fields and click Submit.

Figure 1.26 Click Run The Install.

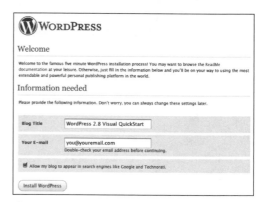

Figure 1.27 Click Install WordPress once you enter this information.

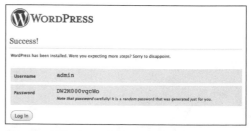

Figure 1.28 WordPress has installed successfully, so you can click Log In to continue.

Figure 1.29 Enter your username and password, and then click Log In.

15. On the login screen, enter **admin** for the username, and then enter the automatically generated password (from step 14). Click Log In to access your WordPress account (**Figure 1.29**).

16. At the top of the dashboard, you should see a highlighted message letting you know that you're using the automatically generated password and giving you the option to change it (**Figure 1.30**). If you're satisfied with the password that was created for you, click No Thanks, Do Not Remind Me Again. If you want to change the password that was created for you, click Yes, Take Me To My Profile Page.

continues on next page

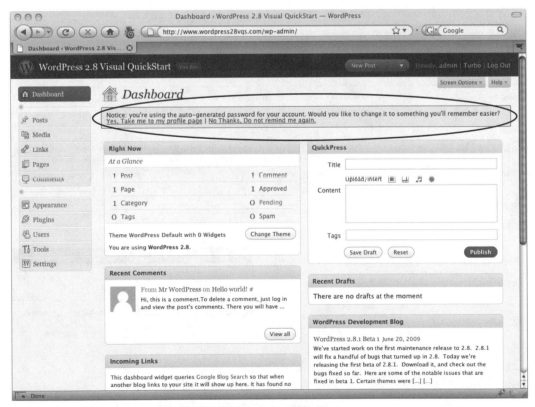

Figure 1.30 To change the password, click Yes, Take Me To My Profile Page.

17. On the profile page, enter your new password twice (**Figure 1.31**). WordPress will help you by letting you know how weak or strong the password you've typed is. When you're satisfied with your password, click Update Profile.

The page will refresh and you should see a confirmation that the user information was updated (**Figure 1.32**). Your password has now been changed. WordPress is set up and ready to be configured.

✔ Tip

■ In case you don't already have an FTP client on your computer, several free clients are available that work quite well. If you use the Firefox browser, you can use the popular FireFTP add-on. For Mac users, Cyberduck is a popular free choice, while LeechFTP is a popular free choice for Windows.

To change your password, enter your new password twice

New Password	••••••••••••	If you would like to change the password type a new one. Otherwise leave this blank.
	••••••••••••	Type your new password again.
	Strong	Hint: The password should be at least seven characters long. To make it stronger, use upper and lower case letters, numbers and symbols like ! " ? $ % ^ &).

Update Profile

Figure 1.31 Changing the password.

Figure 1.32 The user information has been updated.

Get Familiar with WordPress

2

Now is a good time to settle down with WordPress and get comfortable with the way it works. In this chapter, we'll give you an overview of how a WordPress blog functions.

We'll walk you through logging in and navigating the Dashboard, and discuss whether WordPress Turbo is for you. We'll show you how to back up your content and transfer it to and from another blog.

Upgrading from a previous version of WordPress? No problem! We'll talk about upgrading automatically and via FTP to get you up and running as quickly as possible.

How WordPress Works: An Overview

A WordPress site consists of two primary components: the WordPress back-end administration system and the front-end Web site that is displayed to people visiting your site. Both can be customized, but generally the back end is essentially the same across WordPress sites while the front end varies widely based on the design presented in your theme.

When we talk about *using* WordPress, we're usually referring to the back-end system, where content is managed and created.

To log in to WordPress:

1. Many themes provide an easy link on your site for you to use to log in (**Figure 2.1**). If you do not have a login link or would like to navigate there manually, the direct link is your_site.com/wp-admin. If you aren't already logged in, you'll be prompted to do so.

2. Enter your username and password and click Log In to access WordPress (**Figure 2.2**). If you're not on a public or shared computer and would like to save your login information for next time, check the Remember Me check box.

✔ Tip

■ Several plug-ins are available for customizing the WordPress login screen. Using these plug-ins, you can make simple changes, such as modifying the login screen's appearance, to more complex changes, such as allowing OpenID authorization in addition to traditional username/password logins.

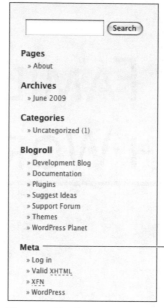

The Meta widget adds a handy login link to your site's sidebar

Figure 2.1 It's often easiest to simply access your WordPress site and log in through the front end.

Figure 2.2 Type your username and password and click Log In.

Finding Your Way Around the Dashboard

The first page you see when you log in to WordPress is the Dashboard (**Figure 2.3**). The Dashboard has several individual modules; the defaults provide a quick way for you to see the current status of your blog, create a quick post, and keep up-to-date on news and information put out by the developers of WordPress.

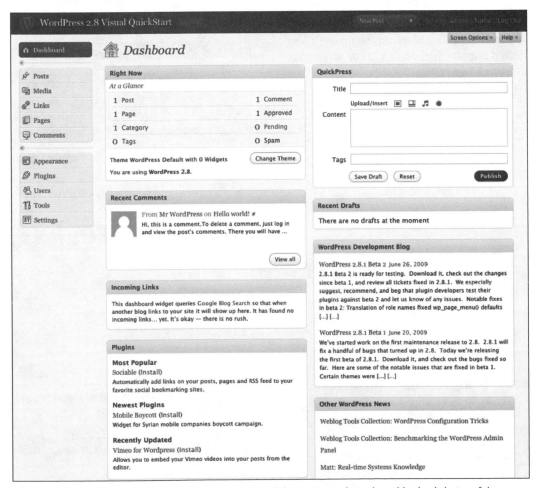

Figure 2.3 The Dashboard gives you quick tools to accomplish common tasks and provides basic but useful information about your site.

◆ The Dashboard button in the left sidebar will be highlighted when you are viewing the Dashboard (**Figure 2.4**).

◆ The Right Now dashboard widget provides a quick list of statistics about your blog: the number of blog posts, pages, categories, and tags as well as information about comments on your blog and the theme you're using (**Figure 2.5**).

◆ QuickPress provides a scaled-down, simple interface to create a new blog post—especially handy if you're in a hurry (**Figure 2.6**).

◆ Recent Drafts will quickly recap any saved but unpublished draft posts or pages you have (**Figure 2.7**).

Figure 2.4 Think of the left sidebar menu as a remote control for your WordPress site.

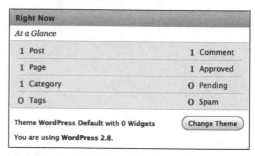

Figure 2.5 The Right Now widget is a quick way to get some basic info about your site.

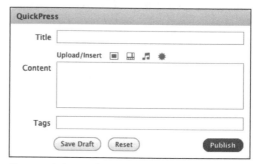

Figure 2.6 The QuickPress dashboard widget lets you make simple blog entries in a hurry.

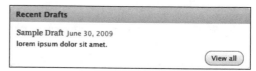

Figure 2.7 Unpublished posts are shown in Recent Drafts.

What Is SEO?

Search engine optimization (SEO) is the process of improving traffic to a Web site by making it more attractive to search engines. Search engines such as Google and Yahoo! use complicated algorithms to compile search results; the more relevant a site appears to search engines, the higher it will appear in the results.

Methods of SEO include adding keywords and phrases to a site's metadata, labeling and tagging posts and images, and coding a site in such a way as to make search engine indexing easier.

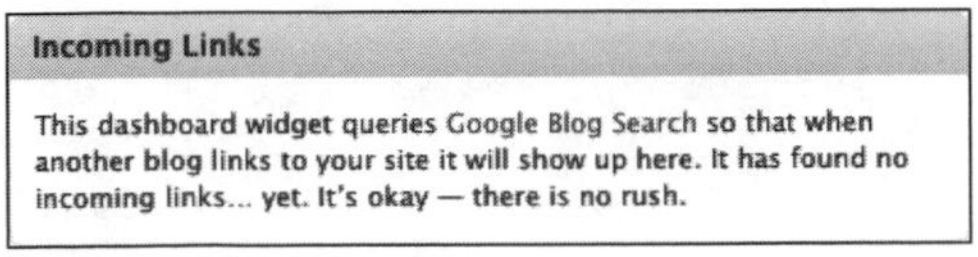

Incoming Links

This dashboard widget queries Google Blog Search so that when another blog links to your site it will show up here. It has found no incoming links... yet. It's okay — there is no rush.

Figure 2.8 Other sites that have recently linked to your WordPress site are shown as Incoming Links.

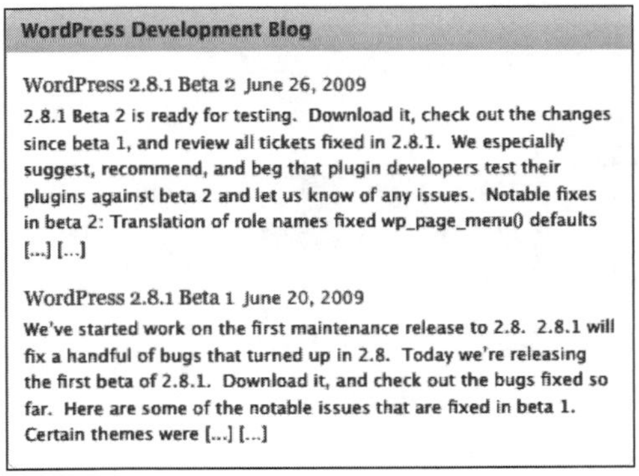

WordPress Development Blog

WordPress 2.8.1 Beta 2 June 26, 2009

2.8.1 Beta 2 is ready for testing. Download it, check out the changes since beta 1, and review all tickets fixed in 2.8.1. We especially suggest, recommend, and beg that plugin developers test their plugins against beta 2 and let us know of any issues. Notable fixes in beta 2: Translation of role names fixed wp_page_menu() defaults [...] [...]

WordPress 2.8.1 Beta 1 June 20, 2009

We've started work on the first maintenance release to 2.8. 2.8.1 will fix a handful of bugs that turned up in 2.8. Today we're releasing the first beta of 2.8.1. Download it, and check out the bugs fixed so far. Here are some of the notable issues that are fixed in beta 1. Certain themes were [...] [...]

Figure 2.9 WordPress Development Blog shows recent posts from the people who make WordPress.

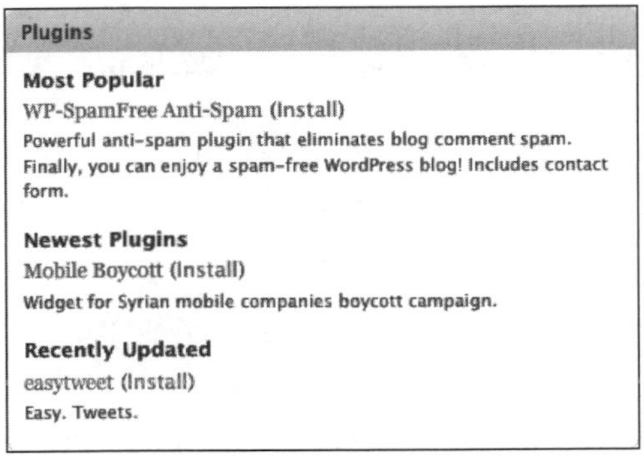

Plugins

Most Popular
WP-SpamFree Anti-Spam (Install)
Powerful anti-spam plugin that eliminates blog comment spam. Finally, you can enjoy a spam-free WordPress blog! Includes contact form.

Newest Plugins
Mobile Boycott (Install)
Widget for Syrian mobile companies boycott campaign.

Recently Updated
easytweet (Install)
Easy. Tweets.

Figure 2.10 The Plugins dashboard widget.

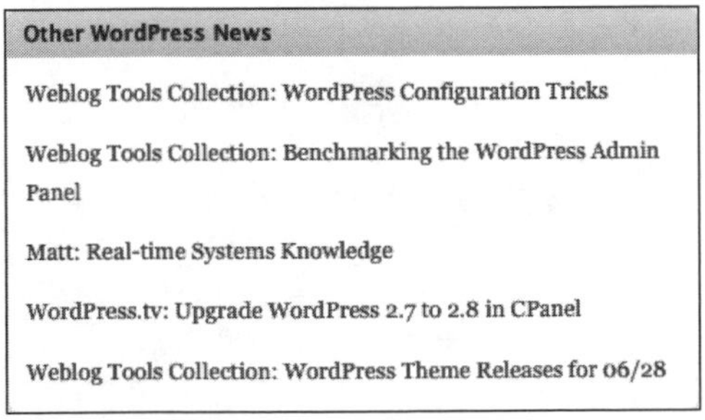

Other WordPress News

Weblog Tools Collection: WordPress Configuration Tricks

Weblog Tools Collection: Benchmarking the WordPress Admin Panel

Matt: Real-time Systems Knowledge

WordPress.tv: Upgrade WordPress 2.7 to 2.8 in CPanel

Weblog Tools Collection: WordPress Theme Releases for 06/28

Figure 2.11 Other WordPress News.

◆ The Incoming Links dashboard widget (**Figure 2.8**) will list any links that people have clicked recently to access your site from other sites. This list can be useful to help you keep track of what people are saying about your posts when they aren't commenting on them directly. Inbound links play an important part in search engine optimization (SEO) so it's a good idea to know who's linking to you. (When you first set up WordPress, of course, there won't be any yet.)

◆ The WordPress Development Blog module (**Figure 2.9**) pulls in recent posts from the developers of WordPress. The full text of these posts can be viewed at wordpress.org/development. Typically these are status announcements about upcoming releases of WordPress.

◆ The Plugins module lists a few new and popular plug-ins that have been added to the WordPress Plugin Directory (**Figure 2.10**). More information about these and other plug-ins can be found by clicking the links in the window or browsing the Plugin Directory at www.wordpress.org/extend/plugins.

◆ The Other WordPress News module (**Figure 2.11**) is similar to the WordPress Development Blog module, but provides links to articles about WordPress on other popular sites such as www.wordpress.tv.

✔ Tips

- Clicking Screen Options at the top right of the screen will cause the Screen Options panel to expand (**Figure 2.12**). You can deselect any of the windows you don't want to see in your Dashboard and adjust the number of columns shown (**Figure 2.13**).

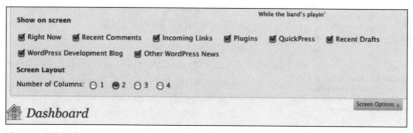

Figure 2.12 The Screen Options panel lets you control which widgets are displayed on your dashboard.

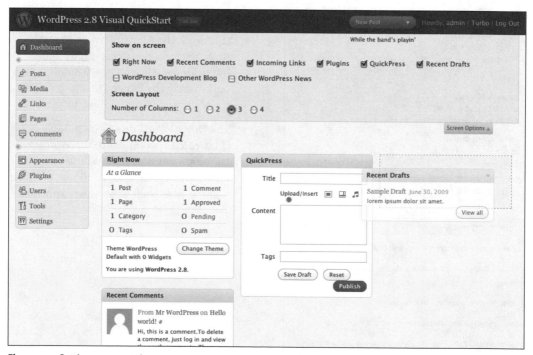

Figure 2.13 Setting screen options.

■ You can also rearrange Dashboard modules by dragging and dropping them into new positions to create a custom Dashboard layout (**Figure 2.14**).

Figure 2.14 You can rearrange your Dashboard widgets.

Using WordPress Turbo

WordPress Turbo is an implementation of Google Gears, a browser plug-in that allows for some of the processing and storage for Web applications to be moved from the Web server to your computer. It will install an icon on your desktop that acts as a shortcut to your WordPress account, as well as store frequently used parts of the application on your computer.

In practice, WordPress Turbo can significantly improve performance, since you won't need to download the stored parts of the application every time you use it.

Browsers have used simple caching mechanisms to attempt some of this same functionality for a long time, but Gears allows for much more offline processing. It uses JavaScript to run in the background without slowing down the browser.

For more information on Google Gears, go to http://gears.google.com.

To set up WordPress Turbo:

1. Click the Turbo link at the top right of the WordPress admin screen to go to the Tools page, where you can begin the installation process for WordPress Turbo (**Figure 2.15**).

Click here to begin installing WordPress Turbo

Click here to access the WordPress Turbo Tools page

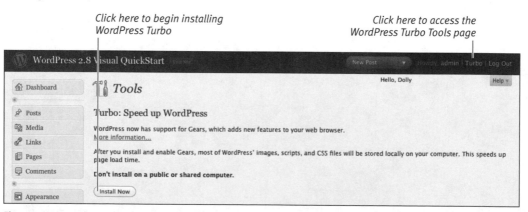

Figure 2.15 Go to the Tools screen to begin the installation process for WordPress Turbo.

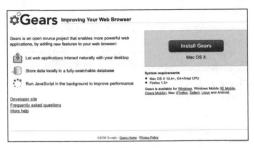

Figure 2.16 When you click Install Now, you're taken to the Google Gears start page.

Figure 2.17 Read the terms of service and click Agree And Download.

Figure 2.18 Google Gears functions as a browser add-on.

2. Click the Install Now button to begin the installation process. You will be taken to the Google Gears site (**Figure 2.16**). Click Install Gears to continue.

3. You'll see the Google Gears Terms of Service; read them and click Agree And Download in the lower-left corner to continue (**Figure 2.17**).

4. Follow the onscreen directions to authorize your browser to use Google Gears (**Figure 2.18**). Our example uses Firefox; other browsers may display slightly different prompts.

continues on next page

USING WORDPRESS TURBO

5. Once Google Gears has been installed, you will need to restart your browser to activate it. Many browsers will provide you with a restart button that you can click to continue (**Figure 2.19**).

6. When you restart your browser, you will most likely be taken back to your Dashboard rather than the Tools page. Click Tools in the left sidebar to continue.

7. On the Tools page, you will see that Google Gears is installed but not yet enabled to work with WordPress. Click Enable Gears to continue (**Figure 2.20**).

8. In the pop-up window that appears, make sure that "I trust this site. Allow it to use Gears" is checked and click Allow to continue (**Figure 2.21**).

9. A counter will be displayed showing the status of the Google Gears update (**Figure 2.22**). Do not close your browser or navigate away from this page while it is running.

10. When the status area reads "Local storage status: Update completed," your installation of WordPress Turbo is finished (**Figure 2.23**).

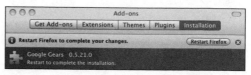

Figure 2.19 You will need to restart your browser to start Google Gears and WordPress Turbo.

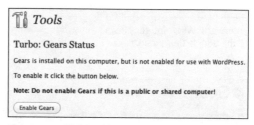

Figure 2.20 Click Enable Gears on the Tools page to continue.

Figure 2.21 Your site will need to be trusted for Gears to function with it.

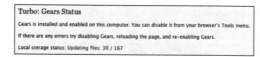

Figure 2.22 WordPress Turbo status.

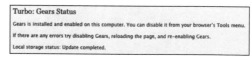

Figure 2.23 WordPress Turbo setup is complete.

Backing Up and Transferring Your Site Content

WordPress provides handy data import and export tools to make it easy for you to migrate posts and other content from one blog to another. These tools offer the quickest and simplest way to generate full or partial backups of your key data.

To export your site content:

1. In the left sidebar of Dashboard, click Tools > Export. You will be taken to the Export Screen (**Figure 2.24**). Click Download Export File to continue.

continues on next page

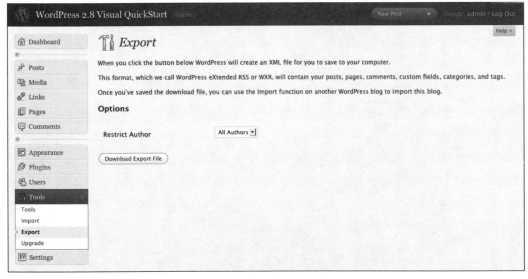

Figure 2.24 Get started exporting your data at the Export screen.

2. WordPress will generate an XML file from your data. Save this file on your computer (**Figure 2.25**).

Your site content has been exported.

✔ Tips

■ Exporting your site creates a record of the content you have put on your site. It's a good idea to export your content periodically as part of your backup strategy.

■ Export does *not* generate a backup of your non-content data or files (such as installed plug-ins and themes). These will need to be backed up separately.

◆ While Export provides a quick and easy way to save records of your content, it cannot substitute for a full backup. Instructions for performing a full backup can be found in the next section, "Backing Up Your Site Data and Files."

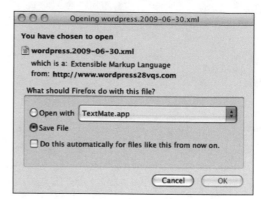

Figure 2.25 Save the export file.

To import site content:

1. In the left sidebar menu, choose Tools > Import to open the Import screen. You'll see a list of all of the various things you can import (**Figure 2.26**). If you want to import data from a previous WordPress export, click WordPress.

Note that you can import content from a wide variety of other sources, but our example uses a previous WordPress export, as is typically used to copy or migrate blog posts from one WordPress site to another.

continues on next page

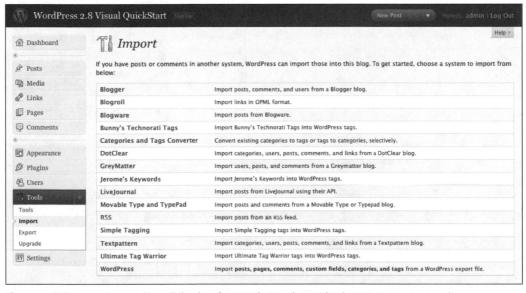

Figure 2.26 The Import screen lists all the data formats that can be used to import content to your site.

2. On the Import WordPress screen, click Browse to locate the exported XML file (**Figure 2.27**).

3. Once you've located the exported file on your computer, select it and click Open to continue (**Figure 2.28**).

4. Click Upload File And Import to start the import process (**Figure 2.29**).

Figure 2.27 Click Browse to locate the exported WordPress extended RSS file (an .xml file).

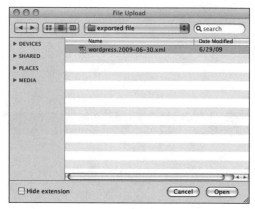

Figure 2.28 Locate the import file and click Open.

Figure 2.29 Upload the WXR file (the .xml file you saved earlier) and import it.

5. The next screen has two additional sections: Assign Authors and Import Attachments (**Figure 2.30**). If you'll be importing data from authors who have accounts on the importing blog, use the drop-down list to match up the user accounts from each blog. If you wish to import attachments (a good idea if you're using this process to migrate your data to a new site), be sure to select the Download And Import File Attachments box. Click Submit to perform the import.

6. A confirmation page will appear telling you what (if any) data was imported (**Figure 2.31**).

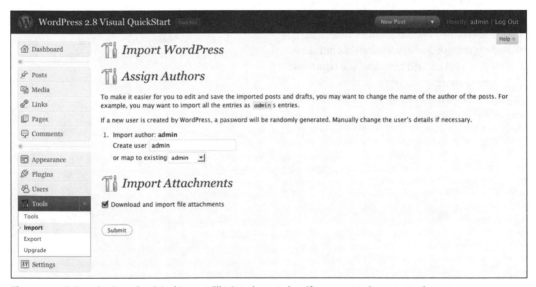

Figure 2.30 Select the Download And Import File Attachments box if you want to import attachments.

Figure 2.31 The import is complete.

Backing Up Your Site Data and Files

Regular backups should already be part of the ongoing maintenance procedure for your computer. You'll want to employ the same principle to make regular backups of your WordPress site.

To do this, you'll need to make copies of two very different things: the data in your MySQL database, and the files that make up your WordPress installation (themes, plug-ins, uploaded images and videos, and so forth).

While there are many ways to do this, we'll show you how to do it with a simple FTP download of the site files, using the popular phpMyAdmin tool to back up your database. If your server or hosting account does not provide phpMyAdmin, you should contact their support staff and check to see what sort of database management tools they offer. Regardless of the tools available, the process should be similar.

You can find a wealth of information on various methods of backing up WordPress on the WordPress Codex site: http://codex.word-press.org/WordPress_Backups (**Figure 2.32**).

To back up your data:

1. Sign in to phpMyAdmin on your hosting account. The URL you'll need to use for this varies from host to host.

continues on next page

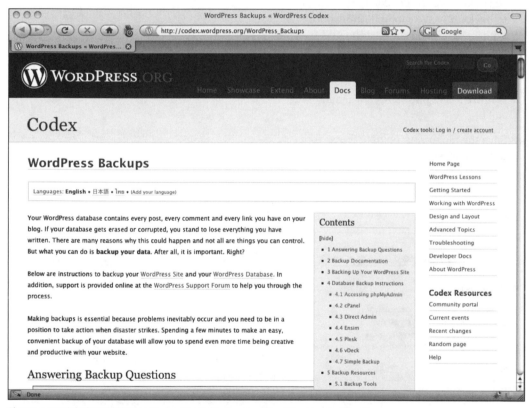

Figure 2.32 Visit the WordPress Codex site to learn more about backing up WordPress.

BACKING UP YOUR SITE DATA AND FILES

2. Click Databases to display a list of databases on your server. The list should include the database you used when you installed WordPress. If you have multiple WordPress sites, you may have stored their data in one or more databases (**Figure 2.33**). Click the Export tab to continue.

3. The next screen contains many fields. Most of these can be left alone, but a few must be filled out. In the Export box, select any WordPress databases you wish to back up. Make sure that the export type is set to SQL, and that the Add DROP TABLE / VIEW / PROCEDURE / FUNCTION and Save As File check boxes are both selected. Click Go to continue (**Figure 2.34**). phpMyAdmin generates a .sql file.

4. Save the file to your computer and your data is backed up. You should now back up your site files.

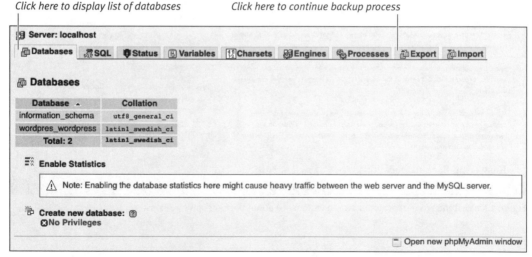

Figure 2.33 The phpMyAdmin databases screen lists all of the databases on your hosting account.

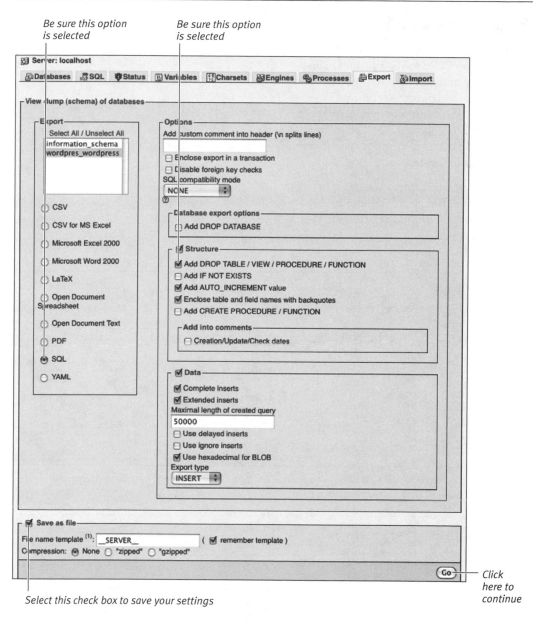

Be sure this option is selected

Be sure this option is selected

Select this check box to save your settings

Click here to continue

Figure 2.34 phpMyAdmin has many options for exporting data.

BACKING UP YOUR SITE DATA AND FILES

To back up your site files:

1. Open your favorite FTP client, enter the settings provided to you by your hosting company, and sign in. You should see a list of files and directories on your Web server as well as on your local computer (**Figure 2.35**). Navigate to the directory where you installed WordPress on your Web host or server.

2. Create a new directory (wordpress in our example) on your computer to which you will download all the site files (**Figure 2.36**).

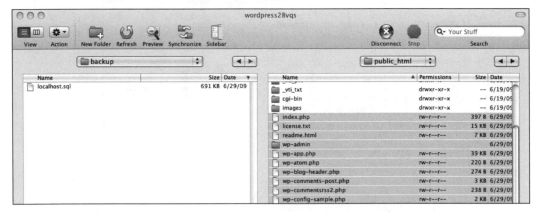

Figure 2.35 This screen contains a list of files and directories on your Web server and on your local computer.

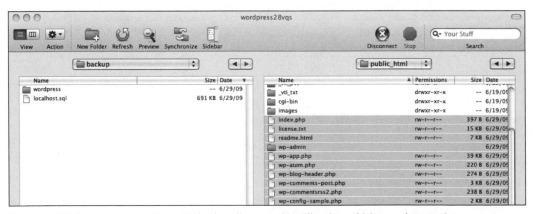

Figure 2.36 It's important to create an FTP backup directory; this will make archiving much neater later on.

3. Drag all of the WordPress files from the server to the directory you created and wait for them to finish downloading (**Figure 2.37**). Most FTP clients will notify you when the job is complete by playing a sound or by displaying a pop-up window.

4. Locate the directory you created on your local computer's file system (**Figure 2.38**).

Notice that we've placed the file directory in the same location as our data backup file (localhost.sql). This way, we can compress them together, which will make restoring the backup much easier if it is needed.

continues on next page

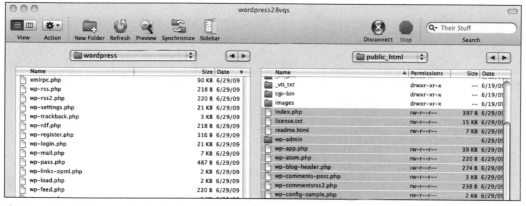

Figure 2.37 The FTP backup files have been downloaded.

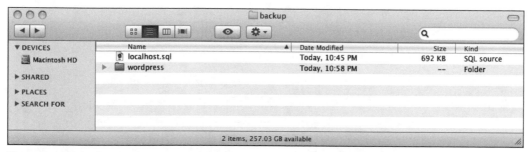

Figure 2.38 The backup directory you created earlier is now full of your site files.

5. Select the files you want to archive and right-click (Ctrl-click on a Mac) to open the context menu. Compress (or archive, or ZIP on some systems) the files to create a zipped file containing both the directory of files and your data backup file (**Figure 2.39**).

The compressed file (Archive.zip in our example) should appear in the directory (**Figure 2.40**). Your backup is complete—just make sure you save that .zip file in case you need it later.

Figure 2.39 Archive (ZIP) your backup.

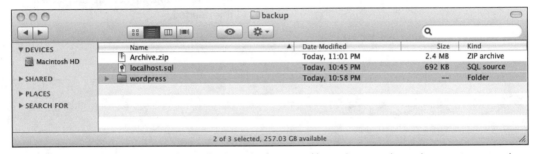

Figure 2.40 The compressed backup files will take up less room and be easier to send to tech support personnel if need be.

Upgrading WordPress

WordPress is always being developed and improved, so it makes sense to keep up-to-date with the latest and greatest version. Luckily, it's easy to upgrade WordPress, whether you're using the automatic upgrade feature available in version 2.7 and higher or upgrading manually via FTP.

To do an automatic upgrade:

1. WordPress 2.7 and above offer automatic upgrades. When a new version of WordPress is released, you'll see a notification at the top of the WordPress admin screen. Click Please Update Now to get started (**Figure 2.41**).

   As always, back up your site files and data before attempting any upgrade.

   continues on next page

Click here to upgrade to new version of WordPress

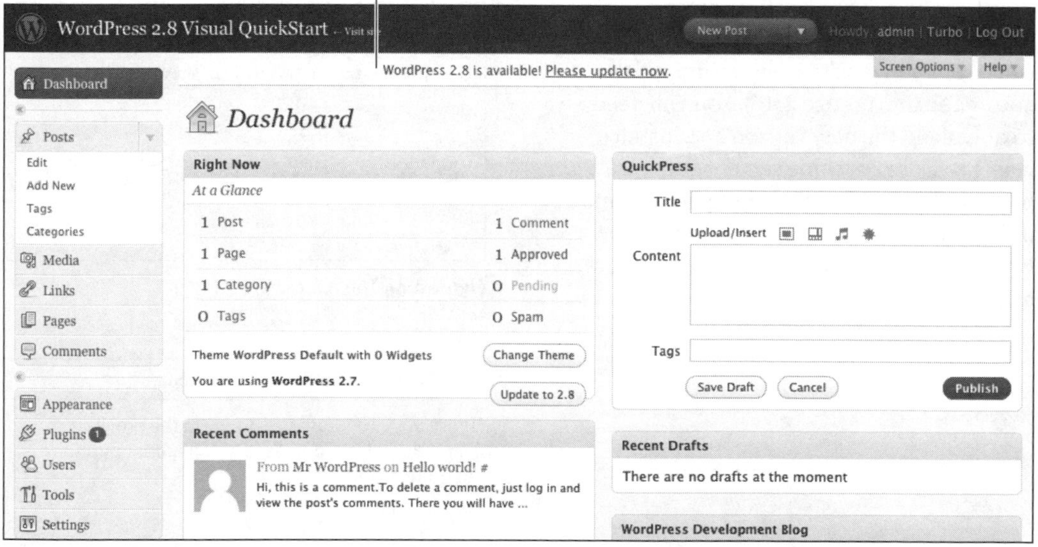

Figure 2.41 The automatic upgrade notice is hard to miss.

2. On the first upgrade screen (**Figure 2.42**) click Upgrade Automatically to start the upgrade process.

3. If your server has the correct permissions set, the upgrade will begin immediately. If your server doesn't allow this, you'll be prompted to supply FTP credentials.

4. Enter the same FTP information that your hosting company provided for you to use with an FTP client. WordPress will attempt to download and install the upgrade using the FTP capabilities of PHP (**Figure 2.43**).

5. When the upgrade is complete, WordPress Upgraded Successfully appears on the screen (**Figure 2.44**).

6. Check your site to make sure that everything is still working. If you have any trouble, take a look at Appendix B, "Troubleshooting," at the end of this book.

If you're upgrading from a version of WordPress prior to 2.7, you may see a notification that a newer version of WordPress exists, but you won't be able to upgrade automatically (**Figure 2.45**). You will need to download the new version and install it via FTP. Likewise, some server setups may prevent the automatic upgrade from running; if that happens, you can still upgrade via FTP. Back up your site files and data before attempting any upgrade.

Figure 2.42 Click Upgrade Automatically.

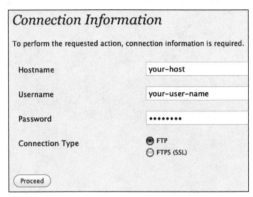

Figure 2.43 You may need to supply your FTP credentials to allow WordPress to add the upgraded files to the server.

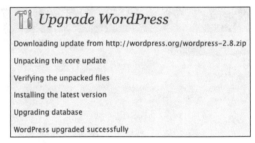

Figure 2.44 The upgrade is complete.

WordPress 2.8 is available! Please update now.

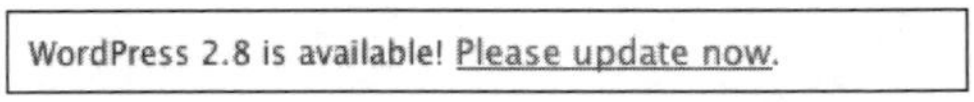

Figure 2.45 The upgrade notice in the previous generation of WordPress is helpful, but upgrading is not quite as easy.

To upgrade via FTP:

1. In your browser go to www.wordpress.org/download and click the Download button on the right of the screen (**Figure 2.46**). A compressed version of the latest version will download to your computer.

2. Save the .zip file to your computer and locate it on your computer (**Figure 2.47**).

continues on next page

Click here to download the newest version of WordPress

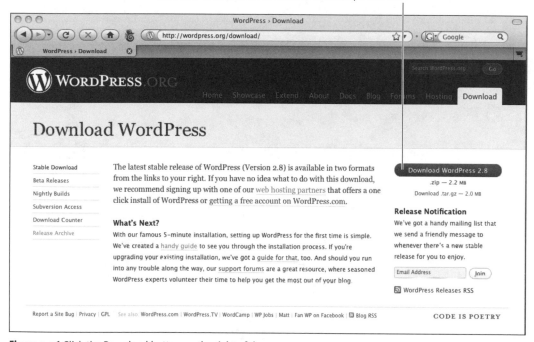

Figure 2.46 Click the Download button on the right of the screen.

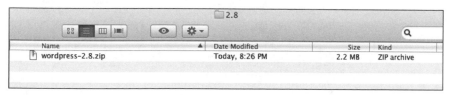

Figure 2.47 Locate the upgrade .zip file.

3. Extract the wordpress directory from the .zip archive by double-clicking the file (**Figure 2.48**).

4. Open your favorite FTP client, enter the settings provided to you by your hosting company, and sign in. You should see a list of files and directories on your Web server as well as on your local computer. Navigate to the wordpress directory on your local computer; then on the server, navigate to the directory in which you installed WordPress (**Figure 2.49**).

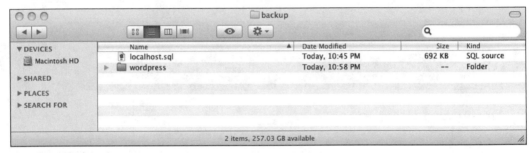

Figure 2.48 Extract the wordpress directory by double-clicking the file.

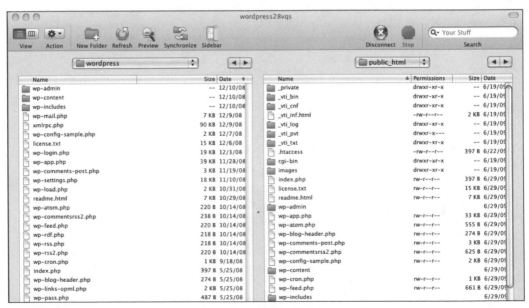

Figure 2.49 Navigate to the directory in which you installed WordPress on your Web server.

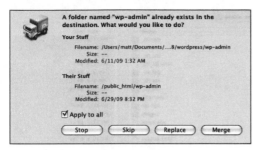

Figure 2.50 Replacing the old files.

Figure 2.51 Log in to WordPress.

5. Select all of the files in the wordpress directory on your local computer and drag them to the server. Most likely you will be asked if you want to replace the files on the server with the ones you're uploading. Select the Apply To All box in your FTP client to apply your choice to all files and click Replace (**Figure 2.50**). This will allow the newer files to overwrite your old WordPress installation with the new version.

6. When all the new files are uploaded, log in to WordPress in your browser to continue the upgrade process (**Figure 2.51**).

7. You'll see the Database Upgrade Required screen. Click Upgrade WordPress Database to continue (**Figure 2.52**).

8. When you see Upgrade Complete, click Continue (**Figure 2.53**).

continues on next page

Figure 2.52 Click Upgrade WordPress Database.

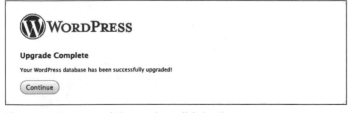

Figure 2.53 Your upgrade is complete; click Continue.

UPGRADING WORDPRESS

9. You'll be taken to the new WordPress admin screens (**Figure 2.54**). WordPress has been upgraded.

10. Check your site to make sure that everything is still working. If you have any trouble, take a look at Appendix B of this book, "Troubleshooting."

Figure 2.54 That's it! WordPress has been upgraded.

MANAGING ACCOUNTS

Accounts in WordPress make it possible for people to access your blog in lots of different ways. You can set up Author and Editor accounts to let other people post articles, Subscriber accounts to make commenting a breeze, and accounts for Administrators, who have the ability to make changes to the theme.

This chapter will give you the lowdown on all the account types and how to use them.

Configuring Your Account

Make your WordPress installation as unique as you are. You can customize everything from your displayed name to the color scheme for the admin screen.

To access your account information:

◆ Click the link with your username at the top right of the WordPress admin screen where the greeting "Howdy, username" appears (**Figure 3.1**).

or

◆ Choose Users > Your Profile in the side-bar menu.

Figure 3.1 Choose either your username or click Users and then Your Profile to edit your account information.

Figure 3.2 Profile options in the Admin screen.

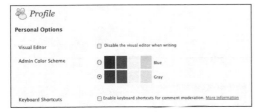

Figure 3.3 Click the link for more information on keyboard shortcuts.

Figure 3.4 You can change everything except your username, and choose a preferred nickname from the drop-down menu.

To make changes to your account:

1. From the profile page, choose among the Personal Options (**Figure 3.2**). You can disable the visual editor when writing, choose a color scheme, and enable keyboard shortcuts for moderating comments (**Figure 3.3**).

2. From the profile page, change the name used to identify you on the WordPress site if you like (**Figure 3.4**).

continues on next page

3. If you wish to provide any additional contact information beyond the required e-mail address to share with the users of the site, add that here as well (**Figure 3.5**).

The About Yourself section is blank by default. You can provide biographical information about yourself that may appear publicly on the site, and you can also use this page to change your WordPress password (**Figure 3.6**).

4. When you have made all your changes or additions, click Update Profile to save them.

✔ Tips

■ If you intend to write your own HTML in the body of your blog posts and pages, disabling the visual editor is a good idea, although most users will find it helpful to leave it on.

■ It's a good idea to enable keyboard shortcuts for comment moderation, giving you a quick way to approve or delete comments.

Figure 3.5 Add as much or as little additional contact information as you like.

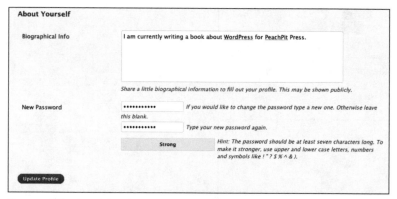

Figure 3.6 The Strength indicator will tell you whether you have chosen a password that would be difficult for a hacker to guess.

Figure 3.7 Click Users to access the list of current user accounts.

Figure 3.8 Current users are listed here.

Managing User Accounts

Whether your blog is a solo affair or a group effort, user accounts make it easy to see who has access to what. You can add new user accounts manually or allow prospective users to add themselves (at an account level you have specified), and you can get rid of troublesome or outdated accounts with just a few clicks.

To add user accounts:

1. Click Users in the sidebar menu to access the list of current user accounts for your WordPress site (**Figure 3.7**). You'll be taken to the Users page (**Figure 3.8**).

2. Click Add New in the Users drop-down menu to add a new user (**Figure 3.9**).

continues on next page

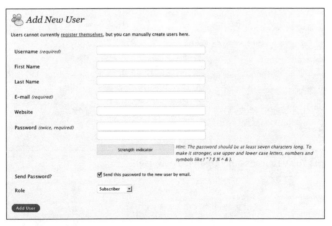

Figure 3.9 The New User screen lets you add a new user.

MANAGING USER ACCOUNTS

3. Enter a username, e-mail address, and password, and then select a role for the new user from the drop-down menu (**Figure 3.10**). Optionally, you may set the user's first and last names and Web site address here.

4. Click Add User to create the account.

You will be taken to a confirmation page where you should see New User Created at the top of the screen (**Figure 3.11**).

✔ Tip

■ If you want to e-mail the new user his account information, select "Send this password to the new user by email" on the screen shown in Figure 3.10.

Figure 3.10 Fill out these fields to create a new user.

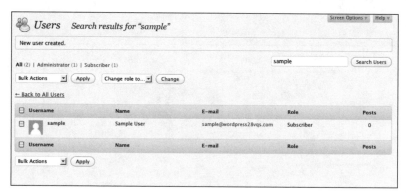

Figure 3.11 You've successfully created a new user!

Figure 3.12 Choose a user and change roles using the drop-down menu.

To change user roles:

1. On the Users page, check the box next to the username of the user whose role you want to change.

2. From the Change Role To drop-down menu, choose the new role (**Figure 3.12**).

3. Click Change when you have made your selection to apply the new role to the selected account(s). Changed Roles should appear at the top of the screen (**Figure 3.13**).

Role changed from Subscriber to Editor

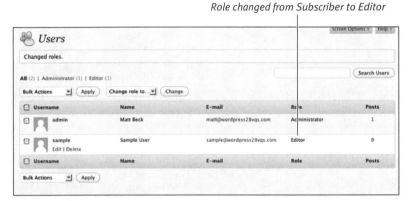

Figure 3.13 Success! You've changed a user's role.

Breakdown of User Account Types

Account types in WordPress are also referred to as *roles*, and they're broken down as follows:

◆ Administrator: This is the Grand Poobah of Account Types, with access to all administrative features, including theme editing and user management.

◆ Editor: Editors can publish and manage their own posts as well as those of other Editors, Authors, or Contributors.

◆ Author: This role gives users the ability to write, manage, and publish their own posts.

◆ Contributor: A Contributor can write and manage his or her own posts, but cannot publish without approval from an Author, Editor, or Administrator.

◆ Subscriber: This type of user can read and comment on posts and receive notification when new articles are posted.

MANAGING USER ACCOUNTS

To edit user profiles:

1. On the Users page, click a username to edit the profile (**Figure 3.14**).

   The process of editing a user's profile is very similar to editing your own profile, but as the admin you can assign user roles in addition to setting general profile information (**Figure 3.15**).

2. After making changes to a user's profile, click Update User at the bottom of the screen.

   A confirmation will appear at the top of the page (**Figure 3.16**).

Figure 3.14 Choose a user to edit.

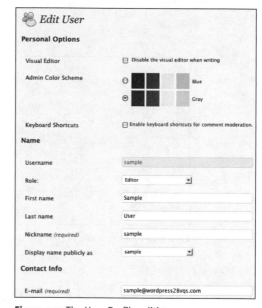

Figure 3.15 The User Profile editing screen.

Figure 3.16 The message User Updated lets you know that your changes have been saved.

> User updated.
> ← Back to Authors and Users

To delete user accounts:

1. Click the Users link in the sidebar and go to the Authors and Users page (**Figure 3.17**). Click the check boxes next to usernames to select the users you wish to delete.

2. From the Bulk Actions drop-down menu, choose Delete (**Figure 3.18**). Click Apply to go to the Delete Users page.

continues on next page

Figure 3.17 Choose users to delete from this list.

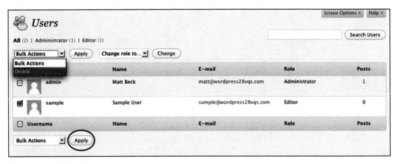

Figure 3.18 Click Apply to continue.

3. You can either delete all of the posts and links associated with the users, or attribute them to another user, such as the admin account (**Figure 3.19**). Click Confirm Deletion.

Back on the Users page, you'll see a confirmation message at the top of the screen telling you how many users were deleted (**Figure 3.20**).

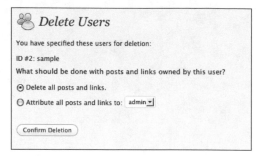

Figure 3.19 Choose an option and confirm deletion.

Figure 3.20 The user has been deleted.

ADDING CONTENT

The most important part of any blog is the content. WordPress gives you the ability to easily update your site whenever you want, making the process of adding posts, pages, images, and media simple and painless.

In this chapter we'll show you the difference between posts and pages; walk you through the process of adding a new post, or editing an existing one; and explain the vagaries of tags, categories, and media files.

Adding Posts

A blog entry or post is time-stamped content displayed in reverse chronological order on a blog. Posts can be assigned to categories or given tags for organizational and archival purposes, and they can include HTML formatting, links, images, and media.

To add a new post:

1. The simplest way to create a new blog post on your WordPress site is to enter the main text into the Content field and a title into the Title field in the QuickPress widget on the Dashboard and click Publish (**Figure 4.1**). If the post is successful, you will see *Post published* at the top of the widget.

   QuickPress is great for quick posts, but since it offers only the options of adding a title, body (with or without media), and tags, anything that requires more customization will need to be done on the Write Posts page.

2. Click Posts in the sidebar menu to access the list of your blog posts (**Figure 4.2**). From here, you can click Add New to access the Write Post subpanel.

3. In the Write Post subpanel, enter a subject for your post, and then enter the content in the body of the post (**Figure 4.3**). Once you've entered a title, you will see a link to the post's URL or *permalink* below the title box. You can change the permalink by clicking the Change Permalink button.

4. Add optional information, such as tags, in the Post Tag section; add or select a category for your post in the Categories section; or add an excerpt for the post in the Excerpt field.

   Tags and categories are covered later in this chapter.

Figure 4.1 The QuickPress widget is the simplest way to add a new blog post.

Figure 4.2 Click Posts in the sidebar menu.

Figure 4.3 Creating a post in the Write Post subpanel.

Figure 4.4
Publishing options. Click the Edit links next to Status, Visibility, and so forth to access additional options.

Figure 4.5 Success! You've published your post.

5. To see what your post will look like on your site, click Preview in the top-right corner (**Figure 4.4**) to open your post in a preview window or tab. You can edit the post's status (draft or pending review) and its visibility (public, password-protected, or private). You can also choose whether to publish immediately or at a later date by clicking the Edit links next to those options.

6. If everything looks good, close the preview window or tab and return to the Write Post subpanel.

7. Click Publish if you are ready to make the post live on your site.

 Once your post is published, you will be taken back to the post editor. You will see *Post published* at the top of the screen, and the window title will be now be Edit Post (**Figure 4.5**). Your post has been published.

 You can continue to edit the post or click View Post to see it on the Web.

To use Quick Edit to edit posts:

1. On any screen of the WordPress admin area, click Posts in the sidebar menu to access the list of posts (**Figure 4.6**).

continues on next page

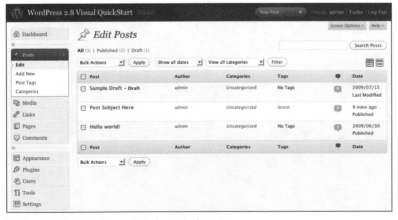

Figure 4.6 A list of both published and draft posts.

2. You can make a quick edit by hovering over the post title in the list and clicking Quick Edit in the menu that appears below the post (**Figure 4.7**).

Quick Edit lets you adjust the metadata for the post, but it doesn't allow you to modify the post body (**Figure 4.8**).

3. You can modify the post title, slug (the URL-friendly name of the post, such as your-post-title), the post date, author, privacy settings, categories, tags, comments, and status of the post.

4. Click Update Post to save your changes.

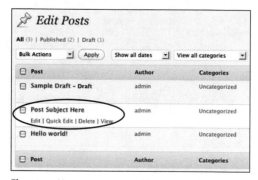

Figure 4.7 Hover over a post title to see the Quick Edit link.

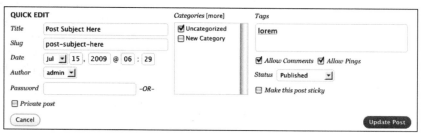

Figure 4.8 Quick Edit is a scaled-down version of the post editor and is useful for making minor changes.

To edit the body of a post:

1. If you want to edit the post body, click Edit instead of Quick Edit to open the Edit Post window (**Figure 4.9**).

2. Using the post editor in its standard visual mode is much like using a word processor to create a document. Click the appropriate toolbar icons to make selected text bold, italic, and so on (**Figure 4.10**).

continues on next page

Figure 4.9 The Edit Post window gives you full control over all aspects of your post.

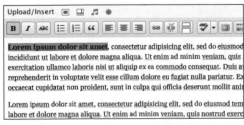

Figure 4.10 Use the icons at the top of the post editor window to format your text.

3. Additional options for styling and adding content are called the "kitchen sink." To access these additional options, click the icon on the far right of the toolbar that looks like a set of dotted lines with a double line below it (**Figure 4.11**).

4. If you want to edit the post's HTML directly, click the HTML tab in the upper-right corner and use the icons in the toolbar (**Figure 4.12**).

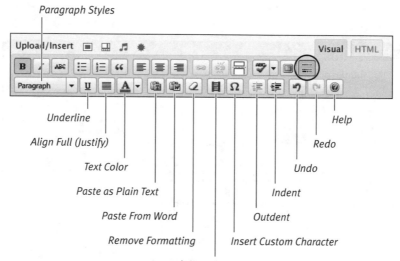

Figure 4.11 Click the icon on the far right of the toolbar to access additional options such as Underline, Highlight, Erase, and Paste From Word.

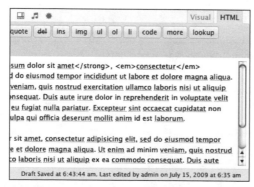

Figure 4.12 You can edit the HTML directly by clicking the HTML tab. This gives you the ability to paste in code snippets that might otherwise be rendered nonsense by the visual editor.

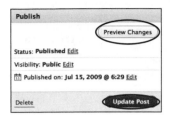

Figure 4.13 Click Preview Changes to view your post exactly as it will look on your site.

5. When you are done making changes to your post, you can preview the changes by clicking Preview Changes, or you can simply click Update Post to apply them directly (**Figure 4.13**).

When the post has been successfully updated, you'll see *Post updated. View post* at the top of the page.

✔ Tip

■ The kitchen sink contains several additional options for manipulating your post. Some of these options, such as Underline, work just like their word processing counterparts. Others provide a more specific function. For example, Paste From Word allows you to paste text that was copied from Microsoft Word without causing formatting problems on your site.

Posts vs. Pages: What's the Difference?

The difference between posts and pages is primarily in the way they are displayed. A post is time-stamped and displayed in reverse chronological order (with the newest at the top) on the main page of your blog. A page, on the other hand, exists outside the normal blog chronology and works best for static information that is less frequently updated, such as a Contact Me page or an About page.

Using Tags

WordPress provides a simple and powerful tagging mechanism for blog posts.

Tags function like mini-categories, providing additional ways for people to find your posts. Tags can also summarize content, which helps search engines determine relevancy.

It is generally a good idea to tag your posts with a few keywords or phrases from the content. So for example, if you write a post about playing tennis with your mother, you might want to tag your post with *tennis* and *mom*. To take it a step further, you might want to tag the entry *sports*, even if you don't use that word in your post.

Those tags will be saved, and if you publish another post tagged with any of your previously used keywords, readers can click the tag to see other related posts. To continue with our example, if you write a post about a racquetball match with your neighbor and tag it *sports*, readers who click that tag will see a list of posts that includes the one in which you played tennis with your mother. It's a great way to link unrelated posts together. Tags don't have to correspond with categories, so you can use them to fine-tune the way your posts are linked together.

To add tags:

1. The easiest method of creating tags is to do it on the fly as you create blog posts using the Post Tags box in the post editor (**Figure 4.14**).

   Replace the text Add New Tag with your new tag and click Add to add it to your post.

2. Add multiple tags all at once by separating them with commas in the list (**Figure 4.15**).

Figure 4.14
Enter tags in the Post Tags box and click Add to append them to your post.

Figure 4.15
Separate multiple tags with commas.

USING TAGS

Figure 4.16
You can choose from your most used tags in the list at the bottom.

Figure 4.17 Blog posts that have been tagged "lorem."

3. To choose from tags you've used in previous posts, click the "Choose from the most used tags in Post Tags" link to expand the list of tags (**Figure 4.16**). As you click the tag names, you will see them appear in the Add New Tag box; click Add to attach them to your post.

✔ Tip

■ Themes implement tags in various ways, but a typical example is the default WordPress theme. Each post has a list of tags in the meta-information at the bottom. When you click a tag on any post, you will see a filtered listing of blog posts that match that tag (**Figure 4.17**).

To manage tags:

1. In the sidebar menu, click Posts, and then select Post Tags to open the window shown in **Figure 4.18**.

You'll see a list of your most commonly used tags at the top, and a list of all your tags on the right. You'll input new tags just below your most commonly used tags.

continues on next page

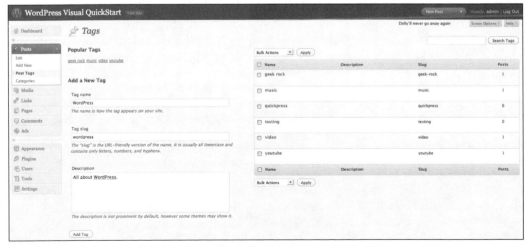

Figure 4.18 All of your tags will be listed here. You can input a new tag using the fields on the left.

2. In the Add a New Tag section, enter a new tag in the Tag name field. The only required field is the tag name.

3. A *slug*, or URL-friendly version of the tag name, will be generated automatically when you click Add Tag. If you want to use a specific URL string, enter it in the Tag Slug field.

4. You can also add a description for your tag. Most themes won't show this, but it can be useful for your own organizational purposes.

   New tags will appear in the list to the right (**Figure 4.19**).

✔ Tip

- From this management screen, you can also remove tags that are no longer relevant to your site by selecting them and choosing Delete from the Bulk Actions drop-down menu (**Figure 4.20**). You must click Apply to delete the tags.

Figure 4.19 Now that you've entered a new tag, you'll see it in the list on the right.

Figure 4.20 Set Bulk Actions to Delete and click Apply to delete selected tags.

Figure 4.21
Choose one or more categories as you create your post using the check boxes to the right of the post editor.

Setting Up and Using Categories

Categories are hierarchical groupings of blog posts, organized by topic. They can be nested, with top-level, or "parent," categories providing the main navigation and an unlimited number of subcategories, or "child" categories, underneath them.

Like tags, categories give users a contextual way to organize and locate the posts on your site. Unlike tags, however, categories can generally be used by your theme or theme widgets to create more powerful navigation for your site than tags can. We delve into theme development more fully in Chapters 8 and 9.

You can add and manage categories using the Categories page in the Admin screen, or add them on the fly as you create posts, just like you do with tags (**Figure 4.21**).

To create and manage categories:

1. Access the Categories page under Posts in the sidebar menu (**Figure 4.22**). You'll see an Add Category section on the left and a list of your current categories on the right.

continues on next page

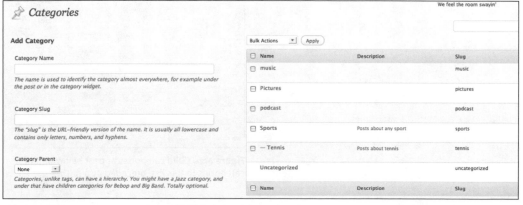

Figure 4.22 Your current categories are listed on the right, and you can enter new ones using the fields on the left.

2. Create new categories by entering a name in the Category Name field (**Figure 4.23**).

3. WordPress automatically generates a category slug when you click Add Tag, but you have the option of entering your own unique URL-friendly identifier in the Category Slug field.

4. You can also choose a parent using the Category Parent drop-down menu.

The default setting is None, which means the new category will be a top-level, or parent, category. If you choose an existing category using the Category Parent drop-down menu, however, the new category will be a subcategory, or child category, of that category.

5. Click the Add Category button to add your new category. New categories will show up in the list on the right, organized by hierarchy with child categories displayed below parent categories with a dash in front of them (**Figure 4.24**).

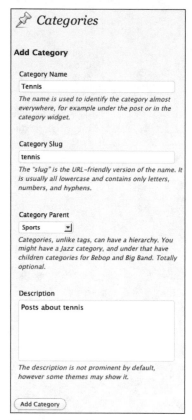

Figure 4.23 To add a new category, all you really need is a name; everything else is optional.

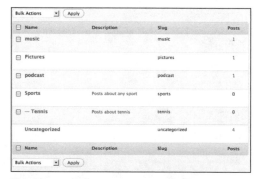

Figure 4.24 Child categories appear below parent categories in this list, preceded by a dash.

Figure 4.25
Add a new category by clicking the Add New Category link in the post editor.

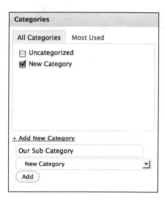

Figure 4.26
Add a subcategory by choosing a parent category from the drop-down list.

Figure 4.27
Your new category will appear in the list.

To create a new category in the post editor:

1. Open the post editor and click Add New Category beneath the list of your current categories (**Figure 4.25**).

2. Enter the new category name and parent (if any) and click Add (**Figure 4.26**).

   You will see a hierarchical list of categories that you can choose from (**Figure 4.27**).

✔ Tip

■ If you want to assign a post to an existing category, just select the corresponding check box and you're done.

Using the Media Library

The Media Library is the place where you can view, edit, manage, and delete your uploaded files. From here you can easily add media to your posts and pages without using a lot of code, and edit details like titles, captions, and thumbnail sizes without re-uploading the file.

To open the Media Library from the Admin area, click Media in the sidebar menu (**Figure 4.28**).

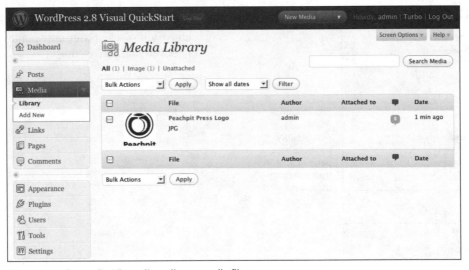

Figure 4.28 The Media Library lists all your media files.

Figure 4.29 Click Media > Add New.

To add new media:

1. Choose Media > Add New in the sidebar menu (**Figure 4.29**).

2. On the Upload New Media page, click Select Files (**Figure 4.30**).

3. Navigate to and choose the file(s) you wish to upload (**Figure 4.31**) and click Select.

continues on next page

Figure 4.30 The Flash uploader on the Upload New Media screen.

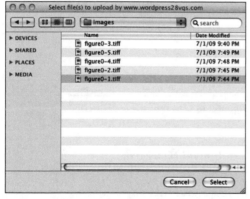

Figure 4.31 Choose the file or files you want to upload from your hard drive and click Select.

USING THE MEDIA LIBRARY

4. When the Flash uploader works, it works great. Unfortunately, it doesn't work properly in all server configurations, so you may see an HTTP error at this stage (**Figure 4.32**). If this happens, don't panic—just click the Browser uploader link.

5. To upload a file using the browser uploader, first click Browse (**Figure 4.33**).

6. Select the file you wish to upload (**Figure 4.34**).

After the file is uploaded, you'll see it listed in the Media Library (**Figure 4.35**).

✔ Tip

■ If you try to upload a file that's simply too large, you may also see an error. In that case, you'll need to contact your hosting provider or upload a smaller file (**Figure 4.36**).

Figure 4.32 An HTTP error in the Flash uploader.

Figure 4.33 Click Browse to locate the file you wish to upload.

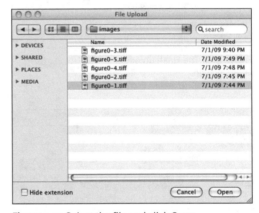

Figure 4.34 Select the file and click Open.

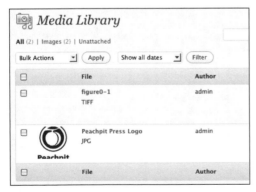

Figure 4.35 Your file is now part of the Media Library.

Figure 4.36 Your file is too big! The note at the bottom will let you know your maximum file size; if you need to upload something larger, contact your hosting provider.

Managing Links

The best way to show the world that you like another blog or site is to link to it. WordPress has a section dedicated to links, making it easy to add, categorize, manage, and publish your links on your blog.

The way your links display on your blog depends largely on your theme and widgets. We talk more about customizing your theme in Chapter 8, "Customizing the Look and Feel."

The first time you click Links in the sidebar menu (**Figure 4.37**), you'll see a list of several links that WordPress installs by default. You'll probably want to remove the default links and start with a clean slate.

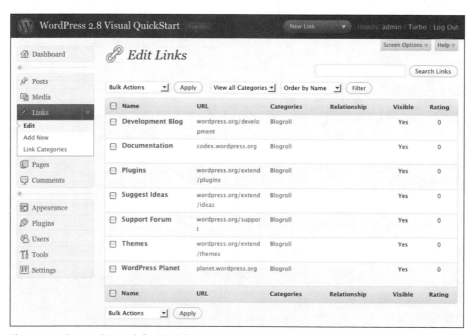

Figure 4.37 The WordPress default link list.

To remove default links:

1. In the sidebar menu, choose Links. On the Edit Links page, click the Name check box to select all the links.

2. Choose Delete from the Bulk Actions drop-down menu (**Figure 4.38**).

   You will see *No links found* where the list was previously. The default links have been removed (**Figure 4.39**).

To add links:

1. Click Links in the sidebar menu.

2. Click Add New to open the Add New Link page.

3. Enter the information for the link you wish to create, including a link category if you want (**Figure 4.40**). Be sure to include the full URL, including http://.

Figure 4.38 Click the Name check box to select all the links in the list.

Figure 4.39 Once the default links have been removed, you can start adding your own.

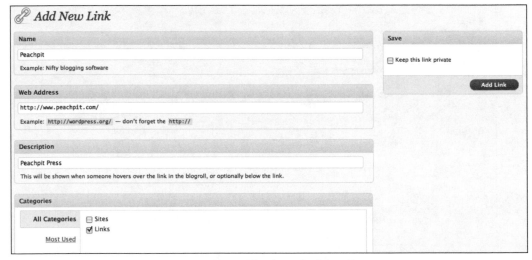

Figure 4.40 Use the full URL of the link you wish to add and give the link a title.

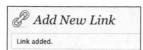

Figure 4.41 Success! Your link has been added.

4. Click Add Link in the Save box on the right, and you should see *Link added* at the top of the page (**Figure 4.41**).

Your link can now be displayed on your site (**Figure 4.42**).

Links can be organized by category, just like blog posts, making it easy to group similar or related links. When your links are assigned to categories, you have the option of displaying specific groups of links on your pages or sidebars, giving you more control over the look and feel of your site.

Figure 4.42 Links are often displayed in a site's sidebar. You can see the link to Peachpit under the "Links" heading.

To add and manage link categories:

1. Select Links > Link Categories in the sidebar menu to open the Link Categories page (**Figure 4.43**). Here you can add, edit, and delete link categories.

Figure 4.43 Manage link categories on the Link Categories page.

Figure 4.44 Name your link category and (optionally) enter a category slug and a description.

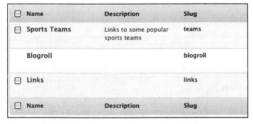

Figure 4.45 A list of categories on the Link Categories page.

2. To add a new category, enter the category name in the Link Category Name field (**Figure 4.44**).

3. WordPress automatically generates a URL-friendly version of the link category name, but if you want to enter your own custom slug, do so in the Link Category Slug section.

4. If you wish, you can also add a description of the link category in the Description field. This may or may not be published on your site, depending on your theme, but it can be useful for your own administrative purposes.

5. To modify a link category on the Link Categories page, find the category you want to modify in the list on the right (**Figure 4.45**).

continues on next page

6. Hover over the link until Quick Edit appears below it. Click it to open the Quick Edit menu (**Figure 4.46**). Alternatively, you can click the link category name to open it in the editor.

7. Make your changes and click Update Category. You will see the changes in the list (**Figure 4.47**).

You can import your computer's bookmarks or links you have bookmarked on a social bookmarking service like Delicious (see the sidebar, "What Is an OPML File?") by using the Import Links feature.

To import links:

1. Choose Tools > Import in the sidebar menu to open the Import page.

2. From the list of import systems, choose Blogroll (**Figure 4.48**).

Figure 4.46 The Quick Edit screen for link categories.

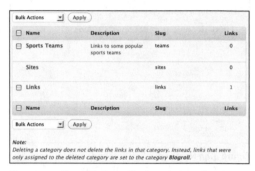

Figure 4.47 Once you've edited a category, the new information will show up in your list of link categories.

Figure 4.48 Choose Blogroll from the list of import systems to import your links.

3. Specify the URL of the OPML file you want to import, or click Browse to find the location of the OPML file on your hard drive (**Figure 4.49**).

4. Choose a category for your links from the drop-down menu.

5. Click Import OPML File to import your bookmarks.

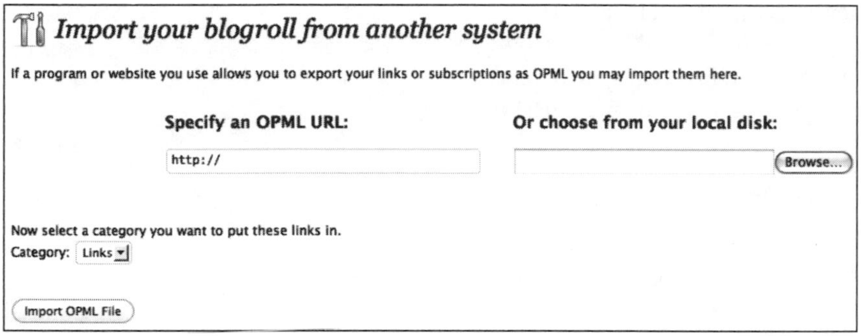

Figure 4.49 Find the OPML file you want to import.

What Is an OPML File?

Outline Processor Markup Language (OPML) is the file format most commonly used for exporting bookmark lists or blog-rolls. OPML uses XML to create an outline that maintains the original organizational structure of the source information, meaning your bookmarks will be grouped the same way after you import them as they were before.

Many social bookmarking services and most browsers have an option to export your bookmarks as an OPML file. If yours offers only HTML export, there are online tools available to convert HTML to OPML, such as the one at BMTD's Yard of Fun: www.smartpeer.net/jiescripts/html2opml.php.

Adding New Pages

Pages are static blocks of content that exist outside the blog chronology. Typically, pages are used for content that is infrequently updated, like an About page or a Contact page. When you update a page, the information isn't added to your RSS feed (learn more about RSS and syndication in Chapter 7, "Syndication").

Adding new pages is almost identical to adding blog posts; both use the same editing tools for content and function nearly identically, so if you're familiar with one, you'll be familiar with the other.

To add a new page:

1. In the sidebar menu, choose Pages > Add New to open the Add New Page subpanel (**Figure 4.50**).

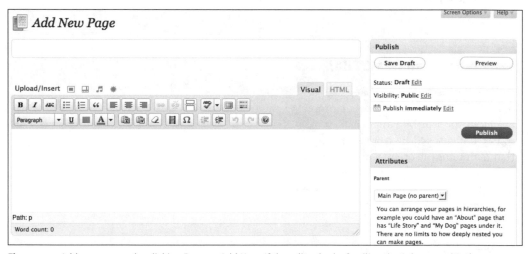

Figure 4.50 Add a new page by clicking Pages > Add New. If the editor looks familiar, that's because it's the same one used to edit posts!

Figure 4.51 You can change the URL of your page by clicking Change Permalinks.

2. Give your page a title. After you type in the page title, a URL, or permalink, will appear below it. You can edit the permalink by clicking the Change Permalinks button (**Figure 4.51**).

3. Add some content to your page. You can format your content using the formatting toolbar at the top of the visual editor (**Figure 4.52**).

4. For more fine-grained control, click the HTML tab to edit the markup of your page.

5. To add media to your page, click one of the icons that appear after the words Upload/Insert at the top of the editor. Learn more about managing media in Chapter 7.

continues on next page

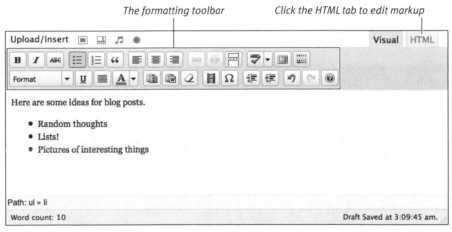

Figure 4.52 Add content just like you would in the post editor; the formatting is the same.

6. Click Publish when you are ready to post the page to your site. You will see "Page published" at the top of the screen (**Figure 4.53**).

Pages are usually used in navigation lists and can be hierarchical, with top-level, or parent, pages making up the main navigation links and subpages, or child pages, as subnavigation. Links are displayed differently depending on your theme; learn more about themes in Chapter 8.

To create subpages:

1. Look in the attributes box on the right of the page editor to see the page hierarchy options. If the page you're creating is an offshoot or secondary to another page, you can choose to make it a subpage.

2. You will need an existing page to function as the parent page. Select a parent in the drop-down menu (**Figure 4.54**). Click Update Page to save your change.

To assign a parent from the page list:

1. Click Pages in the sidebar menu to display the list of pages (**Figure 4.55**). This will open the Edit Pages section, where all your pages are listed.

Figure 4.53 You can view your newly published page by clicking the View Page link next to the Page Published announcement at the top of the screen.

Figure 4.54 Choose an existing page to function as a parent page.

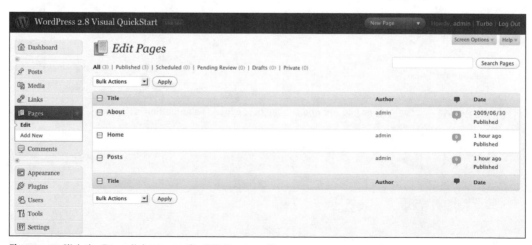

Figure 4.55 Click the Pages link to open the Edit Pages section.

2. Hover over the page you wish to modify and click Quick Edit to open the Quick Edit menu (**Figure 4.56**).

3. Select a parent from the Parent drop-down menu.

4. Click Update Page to save your change.

Your theme can now make use of the page hierarchy you have created to show nested navigation (**Figure 4.57**).

To edit pages:

1. Select Pages in the sidebar menu to open the list of pages (**Figure 4.58**).

continues on next page

Figure 4.56 Use Quick Edit to make changes to a page's hierarchical structure or page order.

Figure 4.57 Nested navigation on a WordPress blog.

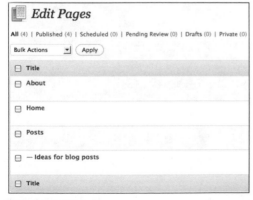

Figure 4.58 A list of your pages.

2. To edit the page's metadata—publish date, author, or page order—hover the mouse over the page title and click Quick Edit to open the Quick Edit menu (**Figure 4.59**).

3. If you need to edit the page content, click Edit.

The process of editing pages is nearly identical to editing blog posts (see "To edit the body of a post" earlier in this chapter for more information on post editing), with the exception of some advanced configuration options, such as page order (see the "How to Control Page Sort Order" sidebar for more information on page order).

4. Once you have edited the page, click Update Page to save your changes (**Figure 4.60**). Your page has been edited.

Figure 4.59 If you don't need to edit a page's actual content, you can use the Quick Edit menu.

Figure 4.60 Success! You've edited your page.

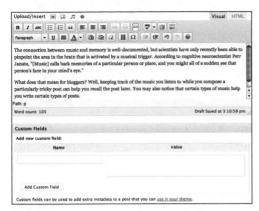

Figure 4.61 The Custom Fields section in the Post Editor.

Using Custom Fields

Custom fields are optional areas in which you can add extra information to your blog posts. For example, you can add a custom field for your mood, or to record the name of the song you were listening to when you wrote your post.

More advanced uses of custom fields depend on your theme or your plug-ins, which can use custom fields for anything from enhanced status updates (what song you're listening to while you write your post, what book you're reading) to more advanced functions such as specially formatted images that go with each post.

If you are already using a theme or plug-in that makes use of custom fields, you can use the Custom Field section in the post editor to add the appropriate content.

To set up custom fields:

1. In the post editor, click Custom Fields to expand the section (**Figure 4.61**).

2. In the Name section, enter the name for your new custom field (for example, Listening To).

3. Enter the value for the custom field in the Value section (for example, Mozart's 5th).

continues on next page

USING CUSTOM FIELDS

4. Click Add Custom Field (**Figure 4.62**).

   Another empty form will appear below your custom field, and the Delete and Update buttons will appear on your custom field, allowing you to edit the information you just added (**Figure 4.63**). The custom field has been added, and if your theme is set up to use custom fields, you will see the fields on your site (**Figure 4.64**).

Custom Fields
Name
Value
Add new custom field:
Name
Value
Listening To
Mozart's 5th
Cancel
Add Custom Field
Custom fields can be used to add extra metadata to a post that you can use in your theme.

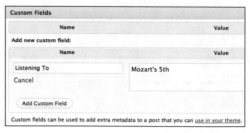

Figure 4.62 Click Add Custom Field to add the custom field to your post.

Custom Fields
Name
Value
Listening To
Mozart's 5th
Delete
Update
Add new custom field:
Name
Value
Cancel
Add Custom Field
Custom fields can be used to add extra metadata to a post that you can use in your theme.

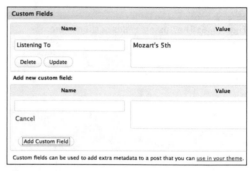

Figure 4.63 Once your custom field has been added, you will see it at the top of the Custom Fields box. The Delete and Update buttons make it easy to edit your previously created fields.

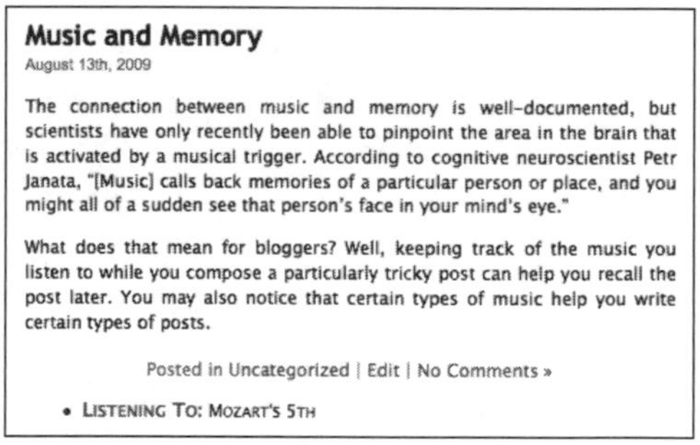

Music and Memory
August 13th, 2009
The connection between music and memory is well-documented, but scientists have only recently been able to pinpoint the area in the brain that is activated by a musical trigger. According to cognitive neuroscientist Petr Janata, "[Music] calls back memories of a particular person or place, and you might all of a sudden see that person's face in your mind's eye."
What does that mean for bloggers? Well, keeping track of the music you listen to while you compose a particularly tricky post can help you recall the post later. You may also notice that certain types of music help you write certain types of posts.
Posted in Uncategorized | Edit | No Comments »
• Listening To: Mozart's 5th

Figure 4.64 This custom field lets the world know what you're listening to.

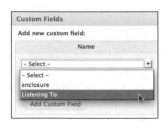

Figure 4.65
In the Custom Fields section, select from the drop-down menu to choose the field you want to update.

To update an existing custom field:

1. Find the link for the Custom Fields section below the post editor and click it to expand the section, if necessary.

2. Choose Select from the drop-down menu in the Name section and choose the field you want to update (**Figure 4.65**).

3. Under "Value" enter the information you want to convey in that field (in this example you'd enter the song you're listening to) and click Add Custom Field.

✔ Tip

■ There are plug-ins such as the My Page Order plug-in that make controlling page order and link order much more user friendly, with a widget-like drag-and-drop interface. Visit http://wordpress.org/extend/plugins/tags/order to see all the available reordering plug-ins.

USING CUSTOM FIELDS

Controlling Page Sort Order

By default, pages on your site will be sorted alphabetically, which is logical, but will often not provide the best way to organize your navigation.

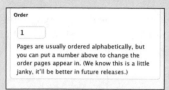

Figure 4.67 Change the order of your pages by numbering them sequentially.

You can change the sort order of your pages manually, however, by assigning numbers to the pages in the Attributes box on the page editor (**Figure 4.66**).

Number the pages sequentially starting at 1. You can do this by editing them or when you create a new page (**Figure 4.67**).

You could also open the Quick Edit menu for each posted page in the page list and set the order there (**Figure 4.68**).

Figure 4.68 Using the Quick Edit menu to change page order.

Figure 4.66 In the Attributes box you can change page order while editing a page.

Managing
Comments

5

One of the great things about a blog is the ability for readers to respond to and interact with both the author and other readers. How do they do this? By commenting, of course!

Comments are enabled by default on a new WordPress blog, but they can be turned off globally or on a per-post level if you want to keep interaction to a minimum. You can also enable comments on static pages.

This chapter will show you how to manage comments on your blog. We'll also show you how to identify and deal with spam, and walk you through the process of setting up Akismet, a popular spam filter created by the same folks who brought you WordPress.

Enabling and Disabling Comments

You can control who is permitted to comment on your posts and pages. You can wield that control on a granular basis, by setting commenting privileges on each post, or globally, by tweaking the settings for your entire site.

To configure comment settings for your site:

1. Click Settings in the sidebar, and then click Discussion to open the Discussion Settings screen (**Figure 5.1**).

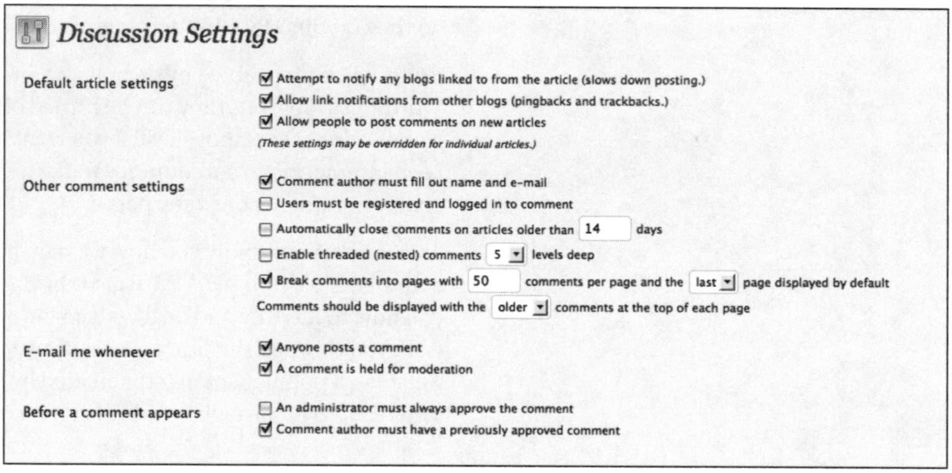

Figure 5.1 The Discussion Settings screen is where you configure the way your site handles comments.

2. Toggle the check boxes to activate or deactivate default discussion settings for your blog. The available options are as follows:

Default article settings: This section lets you decide whether readers are allowed to post comments. Also, you can choose to notify other blogs when you have linked to them in a post, and you can be notified each time another blog links to you—also known as trackbacks and pingbacks (**Figure 5.2**).

Other comment settings: Here's where you can fine-tune the comments on your site. You can require readers to fill out their name and e-mail address before they are allowed to post, and you can also restrict comments to those who are registered and logged in to your site. You can set the amount of time a post will be open for comments (closing comments after two weeks, for example, to minimize spam) and enable readers to have discussions by using threaded comments. You can also choose when to break popular discussions into multiple pages, and whether to display older or newer comments first (**Figure 5.3**).

continues on next page

Default article settings	☑ Attempt to notify any blogs linked to from the article (slows down posting.)
	☑ Allow link notifications from other blogs (pingbacks and trackbacks.)
	☑ Allow people to post comments on new articles
	(These settings may be overridden for individual articles.)

Figure 5.2 Set your default article settings here. You can override these settings on individual posts.

Figure 5.3 Choose how and when comments are displayed in this section.

E-mail me whenever: You can choose to be notified when a comment is posted or held for moderation (**Figure 5.4**).

Before a comment appears: You can automatically hold comments until an administrator has approved them, or automatically approve comments from a reader who has been previously approved (**Figure 5.5**).

Comment Moderation: This section lets you specify limits on links and require moderation for comments containing certain words or phrases (**Figure 5.6**).

E-mail me whenever   ☑ Anyone posts a comment
                          ☑ A comment is held for moderation

Figure 5.4 Set your notification preferences here.

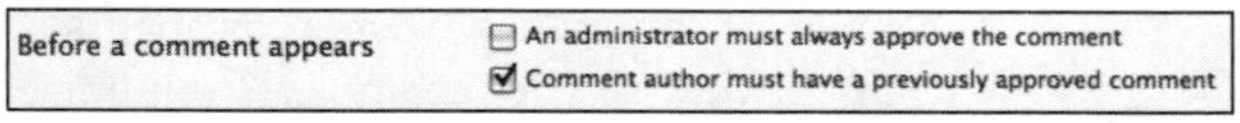

Before a comment appears   ☐ An administrator must always approve the comment
                            ☑ Comment author must have a previously approved comment

Figure 5.5 If you don't want comments from unknown users to go live right away, you can hold them until an administrator has approved them.

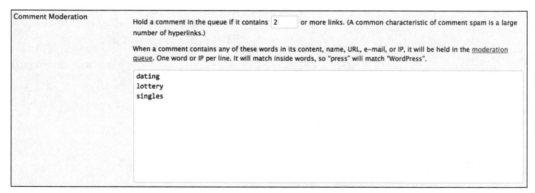

Figure 5.6 If you enter keywords in this section, comments containing the keywords will automatically be held for moderation.

Comment Blacklist: You can automatically flag as spam comments that contain certain words. This option is similar to Comment Moderation but will send blacklisted comments straight to the spam folder rather than holding them for approval (**Figure 5.7**).

Avatars: User pictures or avatars are an optional way for your readers to personalize their posts, and you can enable or disable them here. You can also choose a default for those who do not have an avatar (**Figure 5.8**).

Comment Blacklist	When a comment contains any of these words in its content, name, URL, e-mail, or IP, it will be marked as spam. One word or IP per line. It will match inside words, so "press" will match "WordPress".
	Viagra hacker

Figure 5.7 Comments containing any words or phrases entered in this section will automatically be flagged as spam, so choose keywords wisely!

Avatars

An avatar is an image that follows you from weblog to weblog appearing beside your name when you comment on avatar enabled sites. Here you can enable the display of avatars for people who comment on your blog.

Avatar Display	○ Don't show Avatars ◉ Show Avatars
Maximum Rating	◉ G — Suitable for all audiences ○ PG — Possibly offensive, usually for audiences 13 and above ○ R — Intended for adult audiences above 17 ○ X — Even more mature than above
Default Avatar	For users without a custom avatar of their own, you can either display a generic logo or a generated one based on their e-mail address. ◉ Mystery Man ○ Blank ○ Gravatar Logo ○ Identicon (Generated) ○ Wavatar (Generated) ○ MonsterID (Generated)

Figure 5.8 Choose your default avatar settings here.

To configure comment settings on an individual post or page:

1. After writing a post or page (or from the Edit screen), scroll down to the Discussion box and click to expand it.

2. Toggle the check boxes to allow/disallow comments or trackbacks/pingbacks (**Figure 5.9**).

Figure 5.9 You can override your default comment settings on a per-post basis by toggling these check boxes on a post or page.

Figure 5.10 The Recent Comments widget on the WordPress Dashboard.

Figure 5.11 You can approve, flag, edit, delete, or reply to a comment right from the Dashboard.

Figure 5.12 Replying to a comment from the Dashboard.

Moderating Comments

Once you've received a few comments, you may find that they're not all legitimate. That's where moderation comes in. You can approve, delete, and mark comments as spam to keep your discussions on track. You can also choose to hold new comments in the moderation queue for review before they go live on your site.

To moderate a new comment from the dashboard:

1. Log in to your WordPress site to access the Recent Comments Dashboard widget, which lists the newest comments on your posts (**Figure 5.10**).

2. Hover over a comment in the list to access a simple menu that will let you moderate the comment right from the Dashboard (**Figure 5.11**).

3. Use the tools to modify a comment's approval setting, flag a comment as spam, and edit or delete a comment. You can also click the Reply link to submit a reply to a comment. (**Figure 5.12**).

To edit or approve comments:

1. Click Comments in the left sidebar to view the list of comments (**Figure 5.13**).

   If you have pending comments awaiting moderation, you will see a number in the left sidebar next to Comments (**Figure 5.14**).

2. Click the Pending link on the Edit Comments screen to view the pending comments (**Figure 5.15**).

3. Hover over a pending comment to access the menu of options. You can approve, mark as spam, delete, edit, make quick edits, or reply to the comment.

Figure 5.13 Click Comments in the left sidebar to access your comments.

Figure 5.14 If you have comments awaiting moderation, you will see a number next to the Comments link in the sidebar.

Figure 5.15 Your pending comments are comments that require action before they can be posted on your site.

MODERATING COMMENTS

Figure 5.16 To make quick edits to a comment, hover over it and choose Quick Edit.

Figure 5.17 The Quick Edit screen is a pared-down version of the regular comment editor.

4. To make quick edits to a comment in a comment list, hover over the one you wish to modify and click Quick Edit (**Figure 5.16**).

This Quick Edit feature is similar to the one for blog posts and pages in that it gives you a streamlined version of the regular editor so that you can quickly make a change (**Figure 5.17**).

5. For a more in-depth editing experience, click Edit in the list of options under the comment to open the comment editor. The comment editor allows you to edit the comment's content, just like Quick Edit, but it also lets you set the comment's status (**Figure 5.18**).

continues on next page

Figure 5.18 You can set a comment's status as well as edit its content from the comment editor.

MODERATING COMMENTS

6. After you have made any changes you
need to make, click Update Comment to
save your changes.

If approved, comments are displayed on
your site along with posts (**Figure 5.19**).

Figure 5.19
Approved
comments are
published on
your site.

How to Spot Spam

Spam is the colloquial term for unsolic-
ited and unwelcome messages aimed at
an individual or a Web site, and unfortunately, blogs get their fair share of spam
disguised as comments. Some spam messages are easy to spot, while others might
be confused for actual replies.

Here are some signs that a message is spam:

◆ **Multiple consecutive comments.**
People rarely respond to their own
comments, but spammers often do.

◆ **Keyword-heavy comments.** If a comment uses lots of keywords or a list of
keywords, it is probably spam.

◆ **Links in comments.** A link doesn't
automatically mean that a comment
is spam, but spammers often include
links to drive traffic to other sites.

◆ **Nonsensical or unrelated comments.**
A reply of "Great site, lots of good
information" may seem legitimate, but
if it doesn't directly relate to the post it's
responding to, it may be spam.

Figure 5.20 Click Plugins to begin the process of activating the Akismet plug-in.

Fighting Spam with Akismet

Many plug-ins are available to fight comment spam. One of the most popular is Akismet, a spam fighter that comes bundled with each WordPress installation. It's easy to set up and free of charge, and it was created by Automattic, the company behind WordPress.

To set up Akismet, you will need to get a (free) license key for the Akismet service. The license key comes from WordPress.com, but you don't need to have a blog there in order to use it. In fact, you can set up a single free account on WordPress.com and use the license key (also called an API key) to activate Akismet on several different WordPress blogs.

To set up Akismet:

1. Click the Plugins link in the sidebar (**Figure 5.20**) to view your available plug-ins in the Manage Plugins window.

continues on next page

How Does Akismet Work?

Akismet uses a unique algorithm combined with a community-created database to sort spam comments from legitimate comments. Once you've installed Akismet, each message you mark as spam is added to the community-created database, which helps the plug-in identify similar comments. You can always visit your spam queue to be sure legitimate comments haven't been tagged as spam (**Figure 5.21**).

Figure 5.21 Comments in the spam queue.

FIGHTING SPAM WITH AKISMET

2. Click the Activate link under the listing for Akismet (**Figure 5.22**).

3. Click the "Enter your WordPress.com API key" link that appears near the top of the window (**Figure 5.23**).

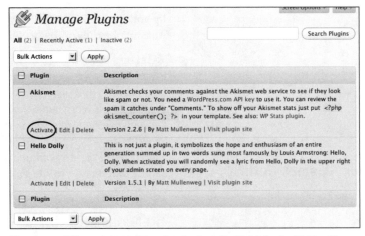

Figure 5.22 Akismet is one of the plug-ins installed by default with WordPress, so you don't need to upload or install anything to access it.

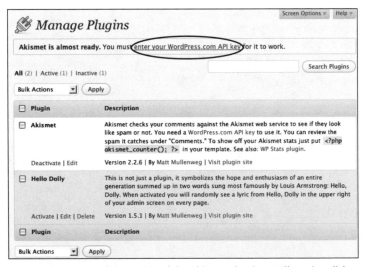

Figure 5.23 Once you have activated the Akismet plug-in, you'll need to click the link that appears at the top of your screen to get a WordPress.com API key.

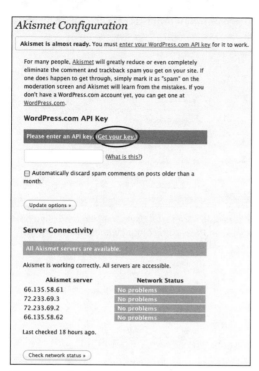

Figure 5.24 The Akismet configuration page requires a WordPress.com API key to work.

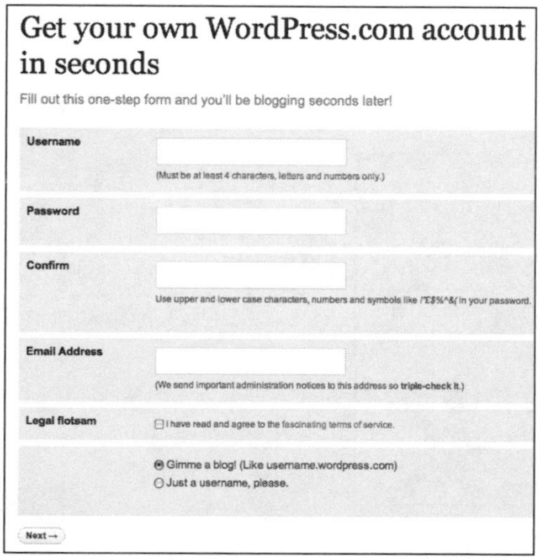

Figure 5.25 Log in or create a new account at WordPress.com to get your API key.

4. On the Akismet configuration page, click the Get Your Key link in the WordPress.com API Key section (**Figure 5.24**). This will take you to the WordPress.com site, where you can get your API key.

   Once you have an API key, you can use it again for any additional WordPress sites you create. You only need one key, even if you have multiple WordPress sites.

5. If you already have an account on WordPress.com, you can log in now to get your API key. If not, you'll need to create an account first (**Figure 5.25**).

continues on next page

FIGHTING SPAM WITH AKISMET

6. Fill out the form with a unique username and password, provide a valid e-mail address, check the box agreeing to the terms of service, and make sure to choose the Just A Username, Please radio button (**Figure 5.26**).

A notification will appear telling you that an e-mail has been sent to the address you just provided (**Figure 5.27**). You will need to activate your account by clicking a link in that e-mail or your account will be removed within two days.

7. In your e-mail inbox, locate the message from WordPress.com. Read the message and click the activation link included (**Figure 5.28**).

You will return to WordPress.com where you will see a confirmation that your account is now active.

Get your own WordPress.com account in seconds

Fill out this one-step form and you'll be blogging seconds later!

Username	WordPressVQS
	(Must be at least 4 characters, letters and numbers only.)
Password	••••••••
Confirm	••••••••
	Use upper and lower case characters, numbers and symbols like !"£$%^&) in your password.
	Password Strength: Good
Email Address	att@wordpress28vqs.com
	(We send important administration notices to this address so triple-check it.)
Legal flotsam	☑ I have read and agree to the fascinating terms of service.

○ Gimme a blog! (like username.wordpress.com)
⦿ Just a username, please.

Next →

Figure 5.26 Click Just A Username, Please to sign up for a WordPress.com account without activating the free WordPress.com blog.

Check Your Email to Complete Registration

An email has been sent to matt@wordpress28vqs.com to activate your account. Check your inbox and click the link in the message. It should arrive within 30 minutes. If you do not activate your account within two days, you will have to sign up again.

Figure 5.27 You will receive an e-mail from WordPress.com with an activation link.

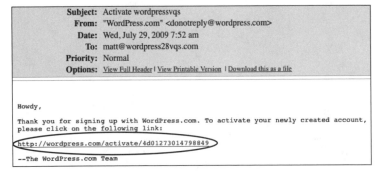

Figure 5.28 Click the activation link from your e-mail to activate your WordPress.com account.

Figure 5.29 Now that your WordPress.com account is active, you will need to log in.

Figure 5.30 Log in to your WordPress.com account.

Figure 5.31 The Dashboard page on WordPress.com is virtually identical to the Dashboard on the self-hosted version.

8. Click Login to continue (**Figure 5.29**).

9. The WordPress.com login screen should look pretty familiar to you, as it matches the one on your site almost exactly. Enter the username and password you created earlier and click Log In (**Figure 5.30**).

You will notice that the WordPress.com Dashboard page looks a lot like your own WordPress site (**Figure 5.31**). You only need to fill out the profile section to set up Akismet.

continues on next page

10. In the left sidebar, click Profile to open your profile page (**Figure 5.32**).

11. At the top of your profile you will see your API key. Write it down, or select the text and copy it to your clipboard (**Figure 5.33**).

12. Return to the Akismet configuration page on your own site, and enter the API key from WordPress.com (**Figure 5.34**).

13. Check the box if you would like Akismet to automatically delete old spam messages (a good idea from a housekeeping perspective), and click Update Options to save your configuration.

Now Akismet will begin cross-referencing your comments against the community database and automatically place suspect comments in the spam queue. You can see the number of spam comments that have been caught by clicking the Akismet Stats link in your sidebar (**Figure 5.35**).

Figure 5.32 Click the Profile link to access your profile page.

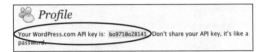

Figure 5.33 Write down, or copy and paste, your API key so that you can enter it on your own site.

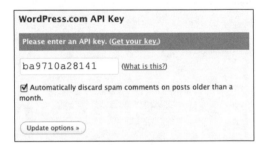

Figure 5.34 Back at your own site, enter the API key to complete activation of the Akismet plug-in.

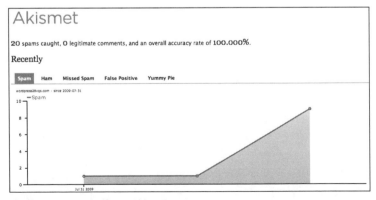

Figure 5.35 A graph of your Akismet spam.

FIGHTING SPAM WITH AKISMET

WORKING WITH MEDIA

Video, audio, images...how do you manage them all? The Media Manager included with WordPress does a great job keeping track of all your media files, providing an easy way to add files and galleries to your pages and posts. In this chapter, we'll show you how to upload and manage your media—whatever the type.

Uploading and Managing Images

Chances are the media files you'll be working with most often will be images. Whether you're posting a few images here and there or running a full-fledged photoblog, it's important to have a quick, easy way to manage your image files.

What is the Media Library?

The WordPress Media Library is the section of your WordPress admin where you can manage your media uploads. Here, you can edit, view, and delete media files. You can select multiple files for bulk deletion, and you can use the Search feature to quickly locate particular uploads.

Media is arranged by date, with the most recently uploaded files appearing first in the list (**Figure 6.1**). An icon at the left of the filename shows you the type of file (a thumbnail for images or a static icon for audio, video, PDF, or .doc files), and at the right you can also see the name of the person who uploaded the file, the post or page it is attached to, the number of comments, and the date the file was uploaded.

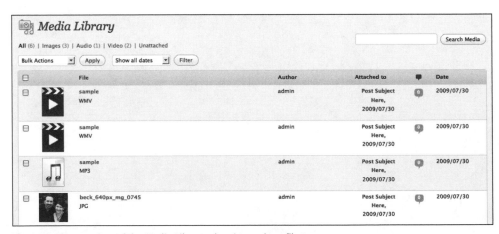

Figure 6.1 An overview of the Media Library, showing various file types.

Figure 6.2 To upload an image to the Media Library, begin by accessing the Media menu in the sidebar.

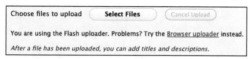

Figure 6.3 Choose the file or files you want to upload. If the Flash uploader doesn't work for you, click the link to use the Browser uploader.

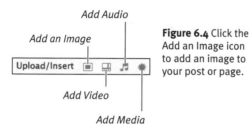

Figure 6.4 Click the Add an Image icon to add an image to your post or page.

To upload an image through the Media Library:

1. Choose Media > Add New in the left side-bar menu (**Figure 6.2**).

2. On the Media Library page, click Select Files (**Figure 6.3**) to open the file selection dialog box.

3. Select the image(s) you wish to upload and click Select.

   A progress bar will show the status of your upload.

   When your image upload is complete, you will be taken back to the Media Library.

To upload an image into a page or a post:

1. In either the Posts or the Pages sidebar, click Add New.

2. At the top of the editing window, you will see the section Upload/Insert and a series of icons. Click the Add an Image icon to open the image uploader (**Figure 6.4**).

continues on next page

UPLOADING AND MANAGING IMAGES

3. Choose the location of your image or images. You can upload files from your computer (**Figure 6.5**), add an image from a URL (**Figure 6.6**), or add an image from your current list of uploaded files already in the Media Library (**Figure 6.7**). Make your choice, change any of the default settings you wish, and click the appropriate button to continue.

4. Finish your post or page as you usually would (you can find more information about posts and pages in Chapter 4, "Adding Content"), and click the Publish button.

Your uploaded image will appear along with your post or page.

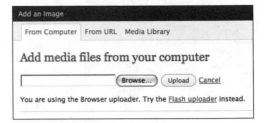

Figure 6.5 Choose an image from your computer to upload into a post or a page, and click Upload to add it.

Figure 6.6 You can add an image from a URL by filling out the image information and clicking the Insert into Post button.

Figure 6.7 Images that have already been uploaded to your Media Library can be added to a post or page by clicking Show, and then clicking the Insert into Post button.

Figure 6.8 When you upload multiple images to a post or page, you will see a new tab, Gallery.

To create a gallery:

1. Create the post or page where you want to add the gallery.

2. Click the Add an Image icon at the top of the edit screen.

3. Upload the files you want to add to your gallery. A ncw tab, Gallery, will appear in the list at the top of the screen, along with the number of images you have uploaded (**Figure 6.8**).

4. Click the Gallery tab. You will see icons of the images you uploaded, as well as options for sort order and gallery settings (**Figure 6.9**).

continues on next page

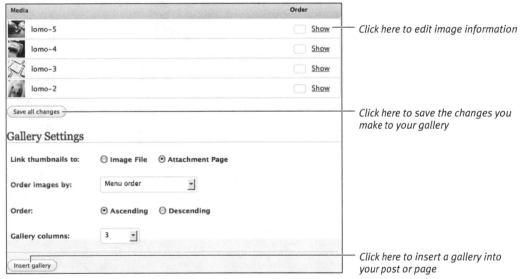

Click here to edit image information

Click here to save the changes you make to your gallery

Click here to insert a gallery into your post or page

Figure 6.9 In the Gallery section of the media uploader, you can control the way your gallery will display on your site.

5. Click the Show link at the far right of each image to edit information for each individual image. When you are done editing, click the Save All Changes button.

6. Under Gallery Settings, choose whether your thumbnails will link to the full-sized image or an attachment page (a blog page with the image on it), the default ordering of your gallery, and the number of columns.

7. Click the Edit Gallery button to insert the gallery into your post or page (**Figure 6.10**).

8. Click the Publish button on the far right to publish the gallery page or post to your site (**Figure 6.11**).

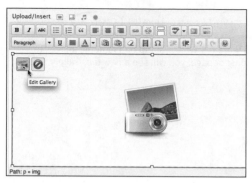

Figure 6.10 A gallery icon in the post editor. You can edit the gallery at any time by clicking the Gallery icon and choosing the Edit Gallery button.

Figure 6.11 A gallery on a WordPress site.

To edit image information:

1. If you're not already in the Media Library, open it by clicking Media in the left sidebar menu. You will see a list of media files. Click the thumbnail image or title of the image you wish to edit.

2. In the Edit Media screen, complete the Title, Caption, and/or Description fields (**Figure 6.12**). You can also view (but not change) the direct URL to your file here.

continues on next page

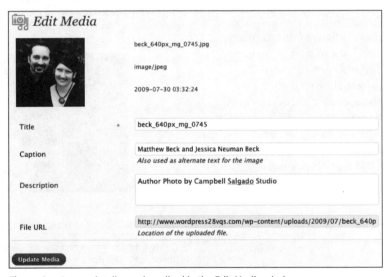

Figure 6.12 Image details can be edited in the Edit Media window.

UPLOADING AND MANAGING IMAGES

Depending on your theme, you can use titles, captions, and descriptions when the image is displayed on your site (**Figure 6.13**). Some themes show an image's details when the image is inserted in a page or a post, some show more details when the image's attachment page is opened (**Figure 6.14**), and others only show the image. Learn more about WordPress themes in Chapter 8, "Customizing the Look and Feel."

3. Click Update Media in the lower-left corner to save your image edits.

✔ Tip

■ Most hosting companies limit the maximum file size that you can upload using PHP (which WordPress relies on). If you are having a hard time uploading a file, try uploading a smaller file, or check with your hosting provider to see if they can assist you with increasing the limit. You are especially likely to encounter this with audio and video files, since they tend to be much larger in terms of file size than images.

Matthew Beck and Jessica Neuman Beck

Figure 6.13 An image with a caption at the bottom. This particular theme displays the caption but only displays the description when the image is clicked.

Matthew Beck and Jessica Neuman Beck

Author Photo by Campbell Salgado Studio

Figure 6.14 The image attachment page, where the image's description is displayed along with the caption.

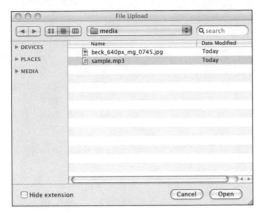

Figure 6.15 Choose an audio file to upload.

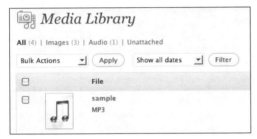

Figure 6.16 Uploaded audio file in the Media Library. The musical note icon helps you quickly identify this file type.

Uploading and Managing Audio Files

Audio files can make your blog more interesting and more interactive. You can upload an audio file of your baby's first words, a lecture, a song, or a piece of music. You can also use WordPress to create a podcast.

Podcasting is fully supported in WordPress and your visitors can even subscribe to your podcasts in iTunes.

To upload an audio file:

1. Follow the steps under "To upload an image," and select your audio file in the File Upload dialog box (**Figure 6.15**).

2. Your uploaded audio file will be shown in the Media Library with a musical note icon (**Figure 6.16**).

To edit audio file information:

1. Open the Media Library by clicking Media in the left sidebar menu. You will see a list of media files. Click the musical note icon or title of the audio file you wish to edit.

2. In the Edit Media screen, fill in or change the Title, Caption, and/or Description fields (**Figure 6.17**). You can also view (but not change) the direct URL to your file here.

3. Click Update Media to save your audio file.

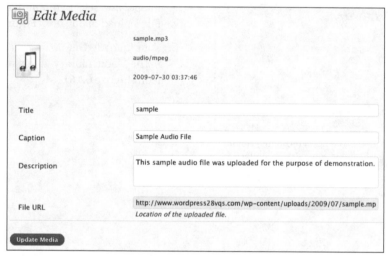

Figure 6.17 Edit the title, caption. and description of your audio file here. You can also see the direct URL to the audio file, which you can copy and paste elsewhere.

Add Audio icon

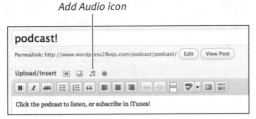

Figure 6.18 The Upload/Insert menu in the post/ page editing screen. Click the musical note to add an audio file.

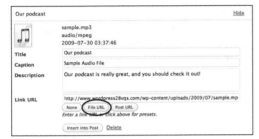

Figure 6.19 Click the File URL button to link directly to your podcast.

To set up a podcast:

1. Open the post editor by clicking Posts in the sidebar and then clicking Add New. This will open the Add A New Post screen.

2. Add a title and any body text you'd like to use, and click the Add Audio icon ♫ to add your audio file (**Figure 6.18**).

3. Edit the file details, specifically the Link URL section—you must click the File URL button to directly link to your audio file (**Figure 6.19**). WordPress will automatically add the necessary enclosure tag to your RSS2 feed to make it usable as a podcast. Click "Insert into Post" to add the audio file to your post.

4. Click the Publish button on the far right to publish your podcast.

✔ Tip

■ Create a category for your podcasts so that users can easily subscribe to just the content they want. We cover categories in Chapter 4, "Adding Content."

Uploading and Managing Video Files

Video files can make your blog more fun and interactive. You can add home movies, training or promotional videos, screencasts—or just share publicly available videos on popular video-sharing sites like YouTube. Follow these instructions for the easiest way to post video on your site.

To upload a video:

1. Choose Media > Add New in the left sidebar menu.

2. On the Media Library page, click Select Files to open the file selection window.

3. Choose the video you wish to upload and click Open (**Figure 6.20**).

   A progress bar will show the status of your upload. Then your uploaded video will appear in the list of uploaded files in the Media Library.

✔ Tip

■ If your file is too large, you will not be able to upload it. Consider compressing your file to make it small enough to upload. Many video-editing programs such as QuickTime give you the option of exporting your file at a lower quality, which will reduce the file size. You can also contact your Web hosting company to find out about increasing file size limits.

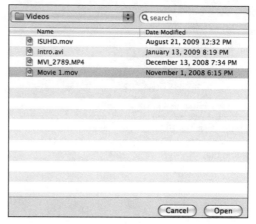

Figure 6.20 Choose the video you wish to upload from this file list.

Figure 6.21
The clapboard slate icon indicates a video file.

To edit video information:

1. Open the Media Library by clicking Media in the left sidebar menu. You will see a list of media files. Click the Add Video icon (**Figure 6.21**) or the title of the video you wish to edit.

2. In the Edit Media screen, fill in or change the Title, Caption, and/or Description fields (**Figure 6.22**).

3. Click Update Media to save your video.

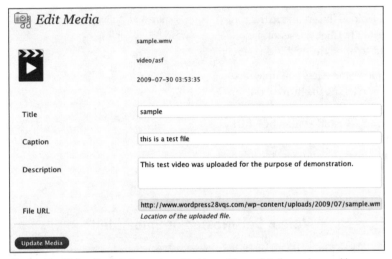

Figure 6.22 Video file details can be edited here. These details can be used by your theme to describe media files in your blog posts or pages.

Adding a Video to a Post

It's easy to add a video to a post or a page, but the procedure differs depending on whether you are hosting the video file yourself or embedding a video from an external video-hosting site such as YouTube.

To add a self-hosted video to a post or a page:

1. Click Add New in either the Posts or Pages sidebar to add a new post or page.

2. While in the Edit screen, locate the icons to the right of Upload/Insert above the tool-bar (**Figure 6.23**). Click the second icon from the left to open the Add Video screen.

3. The Add Video screen lets you upload a new video by clicking the Browse button and finding the video file on your computer. You can also add a video by URL by clicking the From URL tab, or you can click the Media Library tab and select a video you uploaded previously (**Figure 6.24**).

Add Video icon

Figure 6.23 Click the Add Video icon to add a video to your post or page.

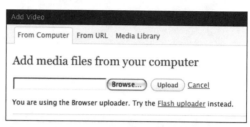

Figure 6.24 Adding a previously uploaded video from the Media Library.

Video: Self-Hosted or Embedded?

Video files are lots of fun, and cameras that record directly to .mp4 or .mov format make it easy to simply upload your files without bothering with a middleman.

Self-hosted video gives you full control over how and when your file is accessible, so if your video contains information about an upcoming product launch or top-secret wedding plans, self-hosting may be more secure.

Hosting videos yourself does have some drawbacks. There are lots of video-hosting services out there (YouTube, Vimeo, and Viddler are three that spring to mind), and once you've uploaded a video to a hosting service, posting it is as simple as pasting the embed code (and there are plug-ins like Viper's Video Quicktags that eliminate even the need to use an embed code). Here are some good reasons to consider using a video-hosting service:

- Video files are large and can take up a lot of space on your server.

- Many video services automatically encode your videos to make them viewable by as many different systems as possible.

- Users can subscribe to your videos either from your blog or directly from the hosting site.

Figure 6.25 Check details before adding to a post or page.

Figure 6.26 A viewed YouTube video with the embed code available.

Figure 6.27 Embed codes are found on YouTube's video page sidebar.

4. Add details to your video, such as a title, description, and caption, and choose whether to link directly to the video or to a page with the video on it (**Figure 6.25**).

5. When you are ready, click Insert into Post to return to the post or page editor.

To add a video to a post or a page using embed code:

1. Locate the embed code for the video you wish to add to your post or page. In this example, embed codes are found in an overlay after the video has played (**Figure 6.26**) and also in a sidebar accessible at all times while viewing the video (**Figure 6.27**). The location of this code varies depending on the video-hosting site; our examples are from YouTube.com.

2. Select the embed code provided by the site and copy it to your clipboard (Ctrl+C in Windows, Command+C on a Mac).

3. Open the post editor and click the HTML tab to access the raw markup for your post.

continues on next page

ADDING A VIDEO TO A POST

4. Paste the embed code into the body of your post (**Figure 6.28**) and click Save.

5. Open your blog page in the browser. It's a good idea to check the post on your site to make sure the video is displaying correctly (**Figure 6.29**).

Adding a Video to a Post

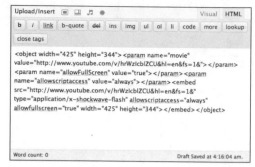

Figure 6.28 Using the HTML tab, add the embed code to your post or page.

Figure 6.29 A post with a video embedded.

SYNDICATION

Once you have some content on your site, you'll want to make it as easy as possible for people to access it. One of the most popular ways for people to follow your posts is to syndicate it with an RSS feed.

WordPress automatically creates an RSS feed for your posts, so all you need to do is configure it to your liking and you're good to go. We'll show you how to set up subscriptions for your posts and comments, and walk you through the process of setting up FeedBurner, one of the most popular RSS feed applications.

Setting Up Your RSS Feed

Really Simple Syndication (RSS) allows frequently updated content to be published in a standardized format. It outputs your new posts in XML so they can be published once and viewed with a variety of programs. This makes it possible for your adoring public to subscribe to your posts with an RSS reader like Google Reader or NetNewsWire. That way, every time you update your site, subscribers will automatically see your new posts.

The RSS logo (**Figure 7.1**) lets your visitors know at a glance that your site has a syndication or RSS feed. Put simply, this allows people to subscribe to your content using a *feed reader*, which is software or a Web application that aggregates several feeds in one place and checks regularly for updates, displaying new content whenever it is found.

To configure your feeds:

1. Choose Settings > Reading in the left sidebar menu to access the feed setting (**Figure 7.2**).

2. At the bottom of the Reading Settings page, choose either Full Text or Summary (**Figure 7.3**).

   If you choose Full Text, entire blog posts will be shown when people read your feed. If you choose Summary, WordPress will display either the excerpt of a post (if you created one—see Chapter 4 for more information on excerpts) or the *teaser*, which consists of the first 55 words of your post.

3. Click Save Changes.

Figure 7.1 The RSS symbol makes it easy to recognize when a site has an available RSS feed.

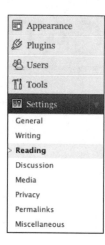

Figure 7.2 Access the Reading settings in the sidebar by clicking the Reading link.

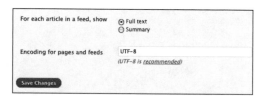

Figure 7.3 Choose whether you want to publish the full text of your posts or a summary in your RSS feed.

✔ Tip

- You can change the text encoding for pages and feeds if you need to use something other than UTF-8 on the Reading Settings page. If you find that your feed comes out with gibberish characters when viewed in a feed reader, you may want to change your encoding. For more information, visit http://phpwact.org/php/i18n/charsets.

Figure 7.4 Click the Widgets link in the sidebar menu.

Figure 7.5 Setting up the Meta widget.

Figure 7.6 The Meta widget adds links to your feeds, your site's admin section, and WordPress.org.

Most themes will include hidden links to your feeds in the header section. These links aren't visible on the page, but applications such as Web browsers will automatically detect the presence of the feed and make it easier for readers to subscribe.

You may want to add more links by using the Meta widget, which automatically adds links to your site's feed in the sidebar, or by displaying an RSS icon on your site. These can make your feed more obvious to visitors to your site and will work for people who use older browsers (which do not automatically detect RSS feeds) as well.

To display your feeds:

1. Choose Appearance > Widgets in the left sidebar menu (**Figure 7.4**).

2. Find the Meta widget (if you're unsure how to use widgets, check out Chapter 9, "Widgets and Plug-ins") and drag it to your widgetized sidebar area (**Figure 7.5**).

3. In Sidebar 1, enter a title if you like, and then click Save at the bottom of the widget.

4. Check your site, and you should see a section in your sidebar that includes links to your feeds as well as other useful links (**Figure 7.6**).

Setting Up Subscriptions

Once you've set up your feed, you or any of your site's visitors can subscribe to it. Subscribing to posts is a great way to keep a record of the articles posted on your blog. Subscribing to comments lets you keep up with ongoing conversations on your blog or follow a discussion you've participated in on another blog. Follow these instructions to subscribe to posts or comments.

To subscribe to your own posts:

1. Copy the link to your feed. Hidden links to feeds in the header of most themes are read by browsers and display in a special location, usually in the address bar (**Figure 7.7**).

   If you have added links to your feeds through widgets or if your theme natively adds links to your feeds in the site body, you can also copy the URL by right-clicking (Control-clicking on a Mac) the feed link and selecting Copy Link from the menu (**Figure 7.8**).

2. In your feed reader of choice, add the feed to your list of subscriptions (**Figure 7.9**).

   All feed readers are set up differently, so check the documentation on your feed reader to learn how to add a subscription. In Google Reader, for example, you add a feed by clicking the Add a Subscription button, pasting the feed URL into the pop-up text box, and clicking the Add button.

   You will now be able to read your blog posts in your feed reader (**Figure 7.10**).

Figure 7.7 Modern browsers will display an RSS feed link in the address bar to let you know a feed is available.

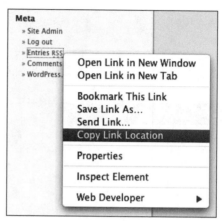

Figure 7.8 Right-click the feed link to copy the link location of the RSS feed.

Figure 7.9 Adding a feed to Google Reader.

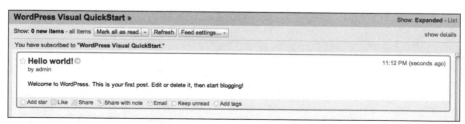

Figure 7.10 Viewing a feed in Google Reader.

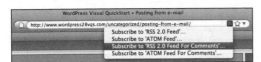

Figure 7.11 A feed to a site's comments is usually available along with a site's post feed.

To subscribe to comments:

1. Click the RSS link in your browser's title bar to find the link to the Comments feed (**Figure 7.11**). You can also find this link in the sidebar Meta widget.

2. Copy the link for the comment feed.

3. Open your favorite RSS feed reader and follow the instructions for adding a new subscription.

   You will now be able to read your comments in your feed reader.

Advanced Uses for RSS

RSS can be used for all sorts of things. Check out these tips for some advanced ways you can use your RSS feed.

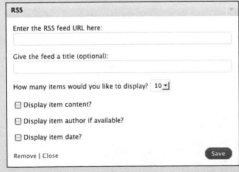

Figure 7.12 You can tweak the RSS widget to display your feed in just the right way.

◆ You can use the RSS widget to add external feeds (or even your own feeds) to your site (**Figure 7.12**). You can combine your external feeds with the Recent Posts or Recent Comments widget to add a second list of feeds with alternate styling.

◆ You can incorporate your Flickr photos or Twitter posts with your blog feed, updating your readers each time you add to those services.

◆ Using WordPress categories, you can create a feed specific to a certain interest, such as podcasting. That way, readers can subscribe only to the posts they want to see.

Using Google FeedBurner with WordPress

Google FeedBurner is one of the most popular Web apps for content redistribution, which is a fancy way of saying that FeedBurner acts as a gateway between your blog and your feed output. Without needing to add any extra code, FeedBurner can give you subscription statistics, support for both XML and ATOM, and lets you incorporate advertising, branding, and multiple source feeds.

If you don't have a Google account, you will need to create one to use FeedBurner.

To create a Google account for FeedBurner:

1. In your browser, navigate to feedburner. google.com. Click Create An Account (**Figure 7.13**).

2. Enter a valid e-mail address and a password in the form (**Figure 7.14**). You can also elect to have FeedBurner keep you signed in, and to enable Web History if you choose.

Figure 7.13 You'll need a Google account to access FeedBurner.

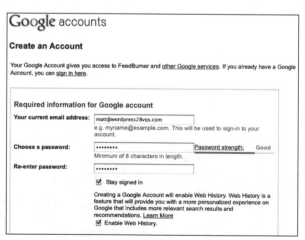

Figure 7.14 Creating a Google account.

Figure 7.15 Accepting the terms of service.

Figure 7.16 Add a blog URL to FeedBurner to begin the process of burning your feed.

Figure 7.17 The FeedBurner-generated Feed Title and Feed Address, which you can customize if you like.

3. Enter the text from the CAPTCHA image (the warped text image that is unreadable by spam bots) in the Word Verification section and click "I accept. Create my account" (**Figure 7.15**).

4. Google will send an e-mail to the address you entered asking you to validate your account. Read the e-mail and click the activation link.

5. You will see a verification screen. You can now log in and add your site to FeedBurner.

To set up FeedBurner:

1. Navigate to feedburner.google.com and log in.

2. In the text box "Burn a feed right this instant," enter the URL to your site, and click Next (**Figure 7.16**).

3. FeedBurner will automatically create a title and address for your new FeedBurner feed. If you don't like the default values, enter new text in the text boxes (**Figure 7.17**). Click Next to continue.

continues on next page

USING GOOGLE FEEDBURNER WITH WORDPRESS

4. You will see a message letting you know your FeedBurner feed is ready to go, and describing its services. Click Next to continue setting up FeedBurner (**Figure 7.18**).

5. Choose the options you want to track with FeedBurner stats (**Figure 7.19**). You can choose to track click-throughs, downloads, individual item views, and more. Click Next once you've chosen all your custom options.

You will see a confirmation screen telling you that you have successfully updated the feed.

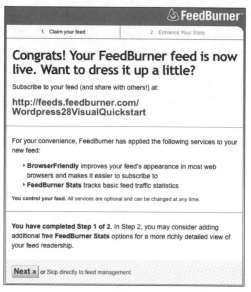

Figure 7.18 FeedBurner success!

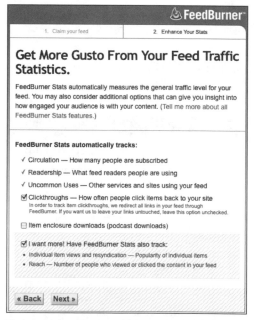

Figure 7.19 FeedBurner tracking setup lets you choose exactly the options you want for your site.

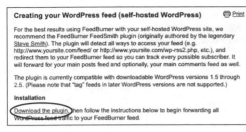

Creating your WordPress feed (self-hosted WordPress)   🖶 Print

For the best results using FeedBurner with your self-hosted WordPress site, we recommend the FeedBurner FeedSmith plugin (originally authored by the legendary Steve Smith). The plugin will detect all ways to access your feed (e.g. http://www.yoursite.com/feed/ or http://www.yoursite.com/wp-rss2.php, etc.), and redirect them to your FeedBurner feed so you can track every possible subscriber. It will forward for your main posts feed and optionally, your main comments feed as well.

The plugin is currently compatible with downloadable WordPress versions 1.5 through 2.5. (Please note that "tag" feeds in later WordPress versions are not supported.)

Installation

Download the plugin, then follow the instructions below to begin forwarding all WordPress feed traffic to your FeedBurner feed.

Figure 7.20 Beneath the instructions for using the FeedBurner plug-in, click the Download the Plugin link to continue installation.

Name	▲	Permissions	Size	Date
_private		drwxr-xr-x	--	6/19
_vti_bin		drwxr-xr-x	--	7/24
_vti_cnf		drwxr-xr-x	--	6/19
_vti_inf.html		-rw-r--r--	2 KB	6/19
_vti_log		drwxr-xr-x	--	6/19
_vti_pvt		drwxr-x---	--	6/19
_vti_txt		drwxr-xr-x	--	6/19
cgi-bin		drwxr-xr-x	--	6/19
images		drwxr-xr-x	--	6/19
index.php		-rw-r--r--	397 B	7/29
license.txt		-rw-r--r--	15 KB	7/29
readme.html		-rw-r--r--	7 KB	7/29
wp-admin		drwxr-xr-x	--	6/30
wp-app.php		-rw-r--r--	40 KB	7/29
wp-atom.php		-rw-r--r--	220 B	7/29
wp-blog-header.php		-rw-r--r--	274 B	7/29
wp-comments-post.php		-rw-r--r--	4 KB	7/29
wp-commentsrss2.php		-rw-r--r--	238 B	7/29
wp-config-sample.php		-rw-r--r--	3 KB	7/29
wp-config.php		-rw-rw-rw-	2 KB	6/30
wp-content		drwxr-xr-x	--	7/29
wp-cron.php		-rw-r--r--	1 KB	7/29
wp-feed.php		-rw-r--r--	220 B	7/29
wp-includes		drwxr-xr-x	--	6/30
wp-links-opml.php		-rw-r--r--	2 KB	7/29
wp-load.php		-rw-r--r--	2 KB	7/29
wp-login.php		-rw-r--r--	21 KB	7/29
wp-mail.php		-rw-r--r--	7 KB	7/29
wp-pass.php		-rw-r--r--	487 B	7/29

Figure 7.21 Navigate to the wp-content folder to find the plug-ins directory.

Name	▲	Permissions	Size	Date
index.php		-rw-r--r--	30 B	7/29
plugins		drwxr-xr-x	--	7/15
themes		drwxr-xr-x	--	6/30
upgrade		drwxr-xr-x	--	7/29
uploads		drwxr-xr-x	--	6/30

Figure 7.22 The plug-ins directory in the wp-content folder.

To incorporate FeedBurner into your WordPress site:

1. In your FeedBurner account, click the Help link at the top right of your screen.

2. Click the link "QuickStart Guides for Blogger, WordPress, TypePad, MySpace, Podcasting," and then click the WordPress link.

3. Under Creating Your WordPress Feed (Self-Hosted WordPress), click the Download the Plugin link to the FeedBurner FeedSmith plug-in for WordPress (**Figure 7.20**). Download the ZIP file and double-click it to expand.

4. Using your FTP client, go to your WordPress install folder and open the wp-content folder (**Figure 7.21**).

5. Inside the wp-content folder you will find the plug-ins directory (**Figure 7.22**). Open the directory in your FTP client.

continues on next page

USING GOOGLE FEEDBURNER WITH WORDPRESS

6. Locate the FeedBurner plug-in on your computer. Upload the entire folder to the plug-ins directory.

7. Log in to your WordPress Dashboard. In your WordPress admin area sidebar, click Plugins (**Figure 7.23**) to view the list of installed plug-ins.

The Manage Plugins page opens.

8. Under FeedBurner FeedSmith, click Activate to turn on the plug-in (**Figure 7.24**).

Figure 7.23 Click Plugins in the sidebar menu.

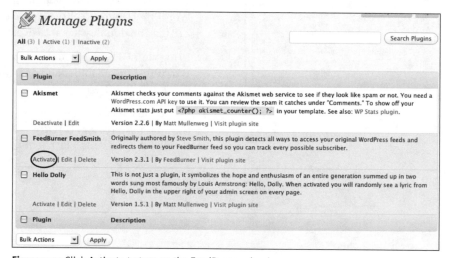

Figure 7.24 Click Activate to turn on the FeedBurner plug-in.

Plugin **activated**.

Figure 7.25 The plug-in is activated!

Figure 7.26 You will see FeedBurner listed in the Settings list. Click the link to set up the FeedBurner FeedSmith plug-in.

The message *Plugin activated* will appear at the top of the list (**Figure 7.25**). You can now configure the FeedBurner plug-in.

To configure the FeedBurner plug-in:

1. In the left sidebar menu, choose Settings > FeedBurner (**Figure 7.26**) to open the setup page.

2. If you have not yet set up your site's feed in FeedBurner, click the link in the first step on the setup page (**Figure 7.27**), or go to feedburner.google.com and follow the steps in the "To set up FeedBurner" section in this chapter. If you've already done this, skip to step 3.

continues on next page

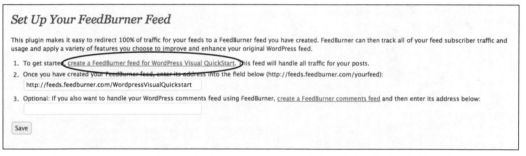

Figure 7.27 If you don't have a FeedBurner feed set up for your site, click the link in the Set Up Your FeedBurner Feed page to get started.

USING GOOGLE FEEDBURNER WITH WORDPRESS

3. Enter the URL of your FeedBurner feed (you can find it by logging in to your FeedBurner account and clicking the name of your site) and click Save (**Figure 7.28**).

The confirmation message *Your settings have been saved* will appear at the top of the page. Your site's feeds will now go through FeedBurner.

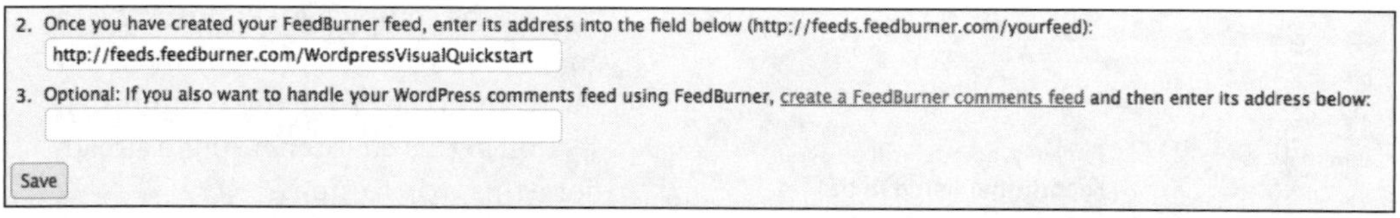

> 2. Once you have created your FeedBurner feed, enter its address into the field below (http://feeds.feedburner.com/yourfeed):
>
> http://feeds.feedburner.com/WordpressVisualQuickstart
>
> 3. Optional: If you also want to handle your WordPress comments feed using FeedBurner, create a FeedBurner comments feed and then enter its address below:
>
> Save

Figure 7.28 Enter your FeedBurner feed in the FeedBurner FeedSmith plug-in to complete setup.

CUSTOMIZING YOUR WORDPRESS THEME

8

One great aspect of WordPress is that you can make it look pretty much however you want it to. You're not limited to a blog-style theme; in fact, many sites use WordPress as a back end without the reader even knowing.

In this chapter, we'll show you how to choose the right theme and give you a peek at the theme editor, which allows you to tweak and edit any theme to your heart's content.

Choosing Your Theme

Your theme will dictate the appearance of your site, including the color scheme, typography, background images, and layout. Some themes even add functionality to your site. For example, you can embed the code for a Flickr badge or automatically import Delicious links. A plethora of free themes is available for WordPress sites, so you can choose one that's just right for you.

✔ Tip

■ A good place to look for free themes is the official WordPress Free Themes Directory at http://wordpress.org/extend/themes/ (**Figure 8.1**).

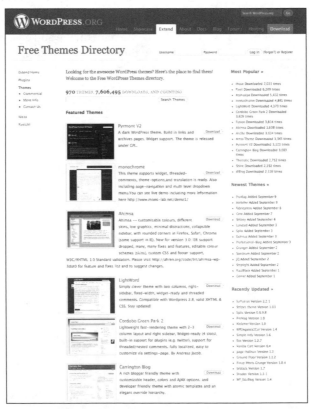

Figure 8.1 The Free Themes Directory on WordPress.org is a great place to find free themes for your site.

CHOOSING YOUR THEME

Figure 8.2 You can access your theme by clicking the Themes link in the Appearance menu.

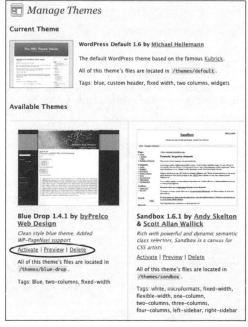

Figure 8.3 On the Manage Themes page, you can see all the themes you have installed on your site. The active theme is on top.

To manage your themes:

1. In the left sidebar menu, choose Appearance > Themes (**Figure 8.2**).

   On the Manage Themes page, you will see a list with thumbnails showing all the themes you have installed. By default, these will be the WordPress Default and WordPress Classic themes, with the WordPress Default theme activated (**Figure 8.3**). Both of these themes come bundled with your WordPress installation and are minimal, blog-style themes. Your currently active theme is shown at the top of the screen. Below each theme, you will see links to activate, preview, or delete the theme.

2. If you'd like to display a different theme, choose it from the list. Click Activate to change your current theme to the new one you have selected.

3. Click Preview to see what your site would look like with that theme by opening it in a pop-up window.

4. If you want to delete a theme, click Delete.

Uploading a New Theme

If you don't want to use the themes that come bundled with your WordPress installation, you can add a new one. You can do so in one of two ways: choosing one through the Dashboard, or uploading one via FTP.

To add themes to your site through the Dashboard:

1. Choose Appearance > Add New Themes in the left sidebar menu (**Figure 8.4**) to access the Install Themes page.

2. Search for a theme by keyword, author, or tag by choosing a search type from the drop-down menu and entering your search term in the text box (**Figure 8.5**).

3. Alternatively, you can use the Feature Filter to assist you with this process by simply checking the boxes that match what features you are looking for (**Figure 8.6**). The Feature Filter can help you narrow down your search results by only showing themes that match your selected colors, columns, width, features, and/or subject. After selecting desired features, click Find Themes.

Figure 8.4 You can add new themes by clicking the Add New Themes link.

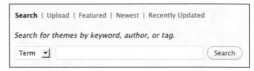

Figure 8.5 Enter search terms to find exactly the theme you want. The drop-down menu on the left lets you choose whether to search by term, author, or tag.

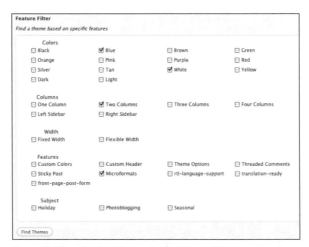

Figure 8.6 Toggle check boxes in the Feature Filter section to refine your search.

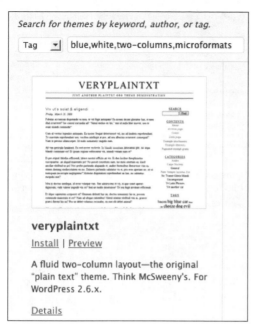

Figure 8.7 Choose a theme from the list and click Install.

Figure 8.8 Click Install Now to install your chosen theme.

4. From the list of themes, find the one you wish to install. Click the Preview link to see a preview of the theme.

5. Once you've decided on a theme, click Install (**Figure 8.7**).

6. In the pop-up window that appears, click Install Now in the lower-right corner to confirm installation of the theme (**Figure 8.8**).

continues on next page

7. Depending on your server configuration, you may need to supply your FTP credentials to allow WordPress to download the required files (**Figure 8.9**). If you see the message "To perform the requested action, connection information is required," you will need to add your FTP hostname, username, and password, and then click Proceed to continue with the installation.

Wait for the words *Successfully installed the theme...* to appear. This will let you know that WordPress has completed downloading and unzipping the theme files (**Figure 8.10**).

8. If you want to activate the theme right away, click Activate.

You will be taken to the Manage Themes page, and you should see a confirmation message at the top of the screen (**Figure 8.11**). The theme will immediately be live on your site.

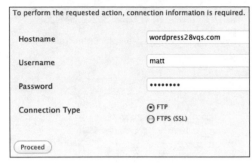

Figure 8.9 You may need to enter your credentials in order to complete the installation of your new theme.

Figure 8.10 Success! Your new theme has been installed.

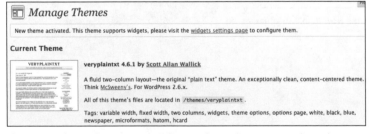

Figure 8.11 The confirmation screen lets you know that your new theme has been activated.

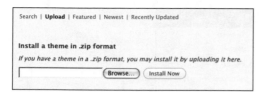

Figure 8.12 Upload a ZIP file containing your new theme.

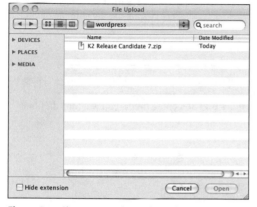

Figure 8.13 Choose your theme from the list of files.

Figure 8.14 Click Install Now.

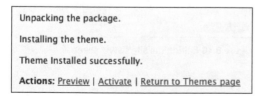

Figure 8.15 Your uploaded ZIP file has been installed on your site.

To upload a theme via FTP from a ZIP file:

1. In the left sidebar menu, choose Appearance > Add New Themes.

2. In the list of links directly below Install Themes, click Upload.

3. Under "Install a theme in .zip format," click Browse (**Figure 8.12**).

4. In the File Upload dialog, locate the ZIP file for the theme you wish to upload. You can use a file you created yourself or one you downloaded from the Internet. Click Open (**Figure 8.13**).

5. When the path to the file is shown in the form, click Install Now (**Figure 8.14**).

6. Wait for *Theme installed successfully* to appear in your WordPress admin area (**Figure 8.15**).

UPLOADING A NEW THEME

Using the Theme Editor

Want to customize that theme? The Theme Editor is the place to do it. Change as little or as much as you want, depending on your skill level and comfort with CSS, PHP, and JavaScript. Novice users can easily modify things like colors, fonts, and backgrounds, while experienced users can access and change any and every aspect of the site.

To use the theme editor:

1. Choose Appearance > Editor in the left sidebar menu (**Figure 8.16**) to open the Edit Themes screen.

2. If you wish to edit a theme other than the currently active theme, select it from the Select Theme To Edit drop-down menu at the top right of your screen (**Figure 8.17**).

   The theme editor will open by default to the style sheet, which is a CSS file typically called style.css (**Figure 8.18**). This file controls the cosmetic aspects of a site, such as fonts, colors, and sizes. More advanced CSS users can also use this file to make extensive changes to a site's layout.

Figure 8.16 You can find the theme editor link in the sidebar.

Figure 8.17 Select the theme you want to edit from the drop-down menu.

Figure 8.18 Editing the site's style sheet.

Theme Files

Templates

404 Template (404.php)

Archives (archive.php)

Archives Page Template
(archives.php)

Comments (comments.php)

Footer (footer.php)

Header (header.php)

Image Attachment Template
(image.php)

Links Page Template
(links.php)

Main Index Template
(index.php)

Page Template (page.php)

Popup Comments
(comments–popup.php)

Search Results (search.php)

Sidebar (sidebar.php)

Single Post (single.php)

Theme Functions
(functions.php)

header–img.php (header–
img.php)

Styles

RTL Stylesheet (rtl.css)

Stylesheet (style.css)

Figure 8.19 On the right of the editing window is a list of available theme files.

3. To the right of the theme editor you will see links to all of the files or *templates* that comprise your chosen theme (**Figure 8.19**). Each file controls a different aspect of your theme, such as the footer, header, main index, and sidebar. Click any of these links to open that file in the edit area.

Novice users should avoid modifying theme files, but if you know a bit of PHP and HTML you can easily access any area you want to change. To make things even easier, WordPress has a handy way to cross-reference PHP commands right from the editor. When you are editing a PHP template file, you will see a Documentation drop-down form appear below the editor (**Figure 8.20**).

continues on next page

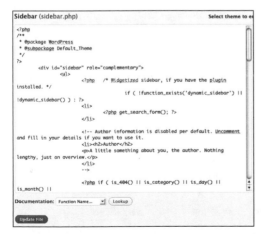

Figure 8.20 Editing the sidebar.php file.

4. Choose from the list of PHP functions that can be used in the templates (**Figure 8.21**).

5. Click Lookup to open a new page that shows the documentation for that function (**Figure 8.22**).

6. Make your changes to the template file and click the Update File button at the bottom of the page.

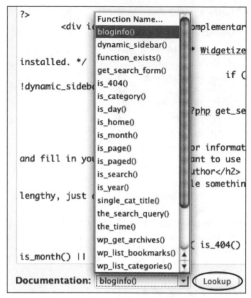

Figure 8.21 Using the Documentation Function Name lookup feature, which gives you a list of available PHP functions.

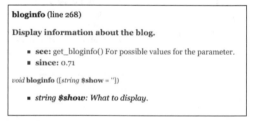

Figure 8.22 Detail of the get_bloginfo() function.

File System Permissions and the Theme Editor

You may run across a situation in which the files for your theme aren't editable by WordPress without additional configuration. In this case, you will see an error message below the edit area (**Figure 8.23**).

> You need to make this file writable before you can save your changes. See *the Codex* for more information.

Figure 8.23 You will need to make this directory writable before you can make changes. Click the link for the Codex to continue.

Changing File Permissions

Languages: **English** • 日本語 • (Add your language)

On computer filesystems, different files and directories have **permissions** that specify who and what can read, write, modify and access them. This is important because WordPress may need access to write to files in your wp-content directory to enable certain functions.

Permission Modes

```
7        5       5
user    group   world
r+w+x   r+x     r+x
4+2+1   4+0+1   4+0+1   = 755
```

The permission mode is computed by adding up the following values for the user, the file group, and for everyone else. The diagram shows how.

- Read 4 – Allowed to read files
- Write 2 – Allowed to write/modify files
- eXecute 1 – Read/write/delete/modify/directory

```
6        4       4
user    group   world
r+w      r       r
4+2+0   4+0+0   4+0+0   = 644
```

Figure 8.24 Changing file permissions information in the WordPress Codex.

Because file system permission management varies widely depending on the server configuration, it is beyond the scope of this book to cover every method. However, this process is well documented at the WordPress Codex. For more information, check out http://codex.wordpress.org/Changing_File_Permissions (**Figure 8.24**).

USING THE THEME EDITOR

WIDGETS AND PLUG-INS

9

Want to add some extra functionality to your site? Widgets and plug-ins are the answer! Widgets and plug-ins extend the functionality of WordPress, allowing you to easily add extra features such as improved menu ordering tools and enhanced customization options, which could be anything from simple contact forms to complex online shopping solutions.

Since plug-ins and widgets are installed separately from your theme, you usually won't need to add any code to your template files to get them to work.

In this chapter, we'll tell you about the difference between widgets and plug-ins, explain how to manage them and use them on your site, and give you an overview of some popular plug-ins.

Widgets vs. Plug-ins: What's the Difference?

The main difference between widgets and plug-ins is the way that they are managed. Widgets have a drag-and-drop interface in the admin area, while plug-ins typically add a configuration screen to the Settings or Appearance area (the location depends on the specific plug-in). Plug-ins are more powerful than widgets, but widgets are easier to use since they require no code and can be arranged and rearranged without modifying your theme.

What are widgets?

Widgets—sometimes called *sidebar widgets* because they are often displayed in the sidebar(s) of your site—are little blocks of self-contained code that you can use to display a wide variety of content on your site. Widgets are essentially specialized plug-ins with a unique WYSIWYG interface. WordPress comes with several widgets by default (see the sidebar "Widgets Included with WordPress"), and you can add other widgets as well by installing plug-ins. Widgets work by providing a content block that can be added to areas of your site (usually the sidebar, although header and footer widgets are becoming more common) that have been predefined by your theme. Widgets are managed using a drag-and-drop interface in the admin area.

What are plug-ins?

Plug-ins are add-on programs that can modify almost any aspect of your site. Some change the way your site functions while others can do anything from adding content from various sources to turning your WordPress site into an e-commerce shopping cart. Unlike widgets, plug-ins may act completely behind the scenes, affecting the operation of your site, rather than adding a simple block of content to it.

You manage plug-ins in the Plugin area of the admin screen, and most installed plug-ins will add a new configuration page to a section of the admin area.

✔ Tip

■ The official WordPress Plugin Directory is a great place to find plug-ins and read feedback on how well they work. You can find the directory http://wordpress.org/extend/plugins/.

WIDGETS VS. PLUG-INS: WHAT'S THE DIFFERENCE?

Using Widgets

Widgets were designed to be as easy as possible to use. Unlike plug-ins, which sometimes require the addition of a line or two of code to your theme, widgets are usable right out of the box and can be managed with a simple drag-and-drop interface.

Figure 9.1 The link to the Widgets admin area in the Admin sidebar.

To use WordPress widgets:

1. In the left sidebar menu, choose Appearance > Widgets to access the Widgets admin area (**Figure 9.1**).

   The Widgets page opens. On the right side of your screen you will see the Sidebar 1 column. (If you have other widgetized areas in your theme, they will be listed here as well.)

2. In the Available Widgets list, locate the widget you wish to add to your site (**Figure 9.2**).

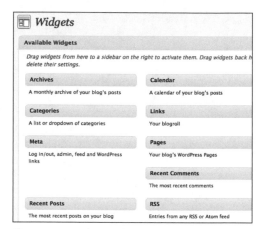

Figure 9.2 Find the widget you want to add to your site.

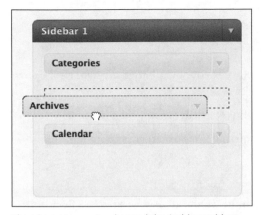

Figure 9.3 Here we've dragged the Archives widget into Sidebar 1, where it will appear between the categories list and the calendar.

Figure 9.4 Customizing the Archives widget by giving it a title and choosing the way the archives are displayed.

3. Choose a widget and drag it to the sidebar and position it where you want it to appear on your site (**Figure 9.3**).

   The widget will expand to show the available configuration options.

4. In the dialog box that opens, choose among any options the widget provides and click Save (**Figure 9.4**).

   The content that corresponds with the saved widget will appear on your site. To add additional widgets, simply repeat this process.

✔ Tips

- You can find an excellent list of available widgets at http://codex.wordpress.org/WordPress_Widgets.

- Some older themes do not include the code required to make use of widgets. If your theme isn't set up to use widgets, take a look at Chapter 10, "Getting Fancy," to read instructions for adding widgets to your theme.

- Widgets are displayed in the order that they are shown in the admin area. You can rearrange them in the Widgets subpanel by clicking a widget's title and holding down the mouse key to drag the widget into whatever order you like.

- You may find that you want to temporarily remove a widget from your site due to seasonal changes or temporary promotions. Fortunately, it's easy to retain that widget for later use.

Widgets Included with WordPress

The following widgets are included with WordPress:

◆ **Archives:** Displays links to the monthly post archive of your blog, either as a list or a drop-down menu.

◆ **Calendar:** Adds a calendar to your site that has links to daily posts.

◆ **Categories:** Adds either a list or drop-down menu that links to category pages and can display the post counts in each.

◆ **Links:** Adds a list of your WordPress links.

◆ **Meta:** Provides links to log in or out, go to the admin screen, access the site's RSS feed, and visit WordPress.org.

◆ **Pages:** Displays a menu of your WordPress pages with the ability to exclude pages and select an ordering method.

◆ **Recent Comments:** Displays up to 15 of the most recent comments made on your site.

◆ **Recent Posts:** Lists up to 15 of your most recent blog posts.

◆ **RSS:** Acts like a mini–RSS reader, pulling in an external feed and displaying the content from it.

◆ **Search:** Provides a simple search form for your site.

◆ **Tag Cloud:** Displays your most frequently used tags in the popular "cloud" format, in which tags are listed in a block with the most commonly used tags displaying in a larger font size than infrequently used tags.

◆ **Text:** Can be used to include on your site static blocks of text or HTML, such as a seasonal ad or promotion in your sidebar.

To disable a widget without losing its settings:

1. Select Appearance > Widgets in the left sidebar menu to access the Widgets subpanel.

2. In the content area on the right side of the screen, locate the widget you wish to disable. Drag it to the Inactive Widgets area (**Figure 9.5**).

   The widget will be removed from your site, but the configuration options will be saved. You can reenable it later by simply dragging the widget back into the content area. You may have any number of inactive widgets saved in this way.

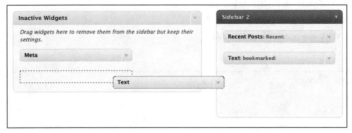

Figure 9.5 The Inactive Widgets area lets you disable a widget without losing any custom settings.

To install new widgets:

1. From the WordPress codex or the widget developer's site, download the widget you wish to install. If the download is a zip file, unzip the file.

2. Upload the entire file or folder to your Plugins directory (located in your installation directory, in wp-content/) (**Figure 9.6**).

3. In your WordPress admin area, click Plugins in the sidebar menu.

The Manage Plugins page opens.

4. In the list, find the widget you just uploaded and click its Activate link (**Figure 9.7**).

The background of your activated widget plug-in will turn white, and you will see the options Deactivate and Edit (**Figure 9.8**).

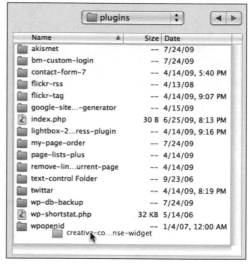

Figure 9.6 Drag the entire widget folder into the Plugins directory.

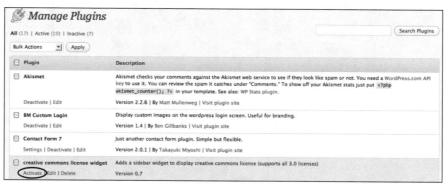

Figure 9.7 Click the Activate link to activate your widget (plug-in).

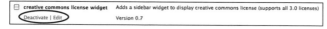

Figure 9.8 The widget has been activated.

USING WIDGETS

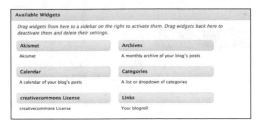

Figure 9.9 Our new widget in the Available Widgets list.

Figure 9.10 Our new widget appears in a blog sidebar below the Recent Posts widget.

5. In the sidebar menu, choose Appearance > Widgets. Your new widget appears in the list of available widgets (**Figure 9.9**).

6. Drag your new widget into the sidebar (or other widgetized area) and fill out the customization options, as outlined in the earlier task "To use WordPress widgets."

Congratulations! You've just added a widget to your site (**Figure 9.10**).

✔ Tip

■ You can configure your widgets through the Widgets subpanel; editing a widget entails modifying the source code of the widget to change its capabilities and is not recommended for novice users.

Using Plug-ins

Plug-ins allow you to add functionality and features not normally included with WordPress, features like drag-and-drop page ordering or integration with third-party sites such as Flickr.com. Each plug-in offers something different, which makes it easy to customize your site.

To add plug-ins to your blog:

1. In the sidebar menu, choose Plugins > Add New (**Figure 9.11**).

   The Install Plugins page opens.

2. Locate the plug-in you wish to add by searching for it by term, author, or tag. Enter your search term in the text field and click Search Plugins (**Figure 9.12**).

3. In the list of search results, find the plug-in you want to install and click Install under Actions, in the right-hand column (**Figure 9.13**).

   Alternately, you can download a plug-in file from a non-WordPress source, usually the plug-in creator's Web site, and follow our instructions for installing a widget (see the "To install new widgets" section in this chapter) to install the plug-in manually.

Figure 9.11 Click Plugins > Add New to add a new plug-in.

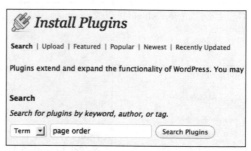

Figure 9.12 Search for a plug-in right from the WordPress plug-in admin area.

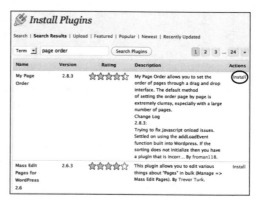

Figure 9.13 Click Install next to the plug-in you want to install.

Figure 9.14 When an information window pops up, click Install Now.

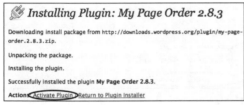

Figure 9.15 Once a plug-in has successfully installed, you can click Activate Plugin to enable it on your site.

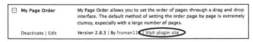

Figure 9.16 Learn more about the plug-in by clicking Visit Plugin Site.

4. In the pop-up window, click Install Now to continue (**Figure 9.14**). The installation process will begin.

5. Once you see the message *Successfully installed the plugin*, click the Activate Plugin link to enable it on your site (**Figure 9.15**).

6. On the resulting screen, click Visit Plugin Site to find documentation, such as development notes and troubleshooting assistance, that is specific to that plug-in (**Figure 9.16**).

✔ Tip

■ Because plug-ins can affect many aspects of your site, their configuration varies. Many, but not all, will add menu options in the left sidebar. Read the documentation for the plug-in you want to use to find out how to configure it.

Plug-ins Included with WordPress

When you first install WordPress, it comes with two plug-ins right out of the box: Akismet and Hello Dolly.

◆ **Akismet:** The Akismet plug-in is an excellent tool for combating spam comments on your blog. For detailed instructions on using Akismet, refer to Chapter 5, Managing Comments." To learn more about Akismet, go to http://akismet.com.

◆ **Hello Dolly:** The first official WordPress plug-in, Hello Dolly, doesn't really do much. If you activate it, a random lyric from the Broadway musical *Hello Dolly* will appear at the top right of your admin screen. This simple plug-in is provided in part as a basic example for plug-in developers.

Upgrading Plug-ins

If a number appears next to Plugins in the sidebar menu, that means you have plug-ins that have available upgrades (**Figure 9.17**).

To upgrade plug-ins:

1. Select Plugins from the left sidebar menu. When you see a notice that a new version of your plug-in is available, you can automatically upgrade the plug-in (**Figure 9.18**).

2. Click Upgrade Automatically to continue. The update will automatically install in WordPress.

   When you see the message *Plugin reactivated successfully*, that means your plug-in is up-to-date and reactivated (**Figure 9.19**).

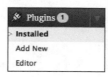

Figure 9.17 A small red circle containing a number next to Plugins in the sidebar lets you know that upgrades are available.

Figure 9.18 Automatically upgrade your plug-in by clicking Upgrade Automatically.

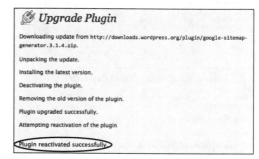

Figure 9.19 Once your plug-in has updated, it will reactivate automatically.

GETTING FANCY WITH THEMES

10

So you know a little HTML and Cascading Style Sheets (CSS) and you want to make your theme a little less...generic? This is the chapter for you. We'll walk you through the process of making some modifications to the default WordPress theme, Kubrick, which features a blue header, a sidebar, and a pretty conventional layout. The areas we'll be making changes to in this chapter are the header and the sidebar. We'll also be adding widgets to a theme that isn't widget enabled, using CSS to make some basic color scheme and font changes to your theme and setting up a favicon, a tiny icon that appears next to a URL in most modern browsers.

Changing a Theme's Appearance

Modifying a theme can be a great way to add a bit of customization to your page. In Chapter 8 we showed you how to use the Theme Editor to access your theme's template files. This chapter will walk you through the process of making some changes to those files. The amount you're comfortable modifying depends on your comfort level with HTML, CSS, and PHP (although much of the PHP is just cut and paste). With only a basic knowledge of Web site coding, you can make striking changes to your site's appearance.

✔ Tip

- If you're not familiar with HTML or CSS, check out *HTML, XHTML, and CSS, Sixth Edition: Visual QuickStart Guide* by Elizabeth Castro (Peachpit Press, 2006) to learn more.

HTML: A Basic Primer

HTML is a series of tags that are integrated with the text of your Web site. These tags are not visible to your viewers, but they tell browsers how to handle the information on your site.

HTML tags always have a beginning and an ending. For example, if you see a <table> tag, there will need to be a closing </table> tag at the end of that section.

You will encounter a lot of HTML tags when working with your WordPress theme files, but to get you started we'll list some commonly used tags and explain what they mean:

- ◆ <title> is the title of your page and displays in the top of the browser.

- ◆ <h1> represents *headline 1*, and it is the largest and most important headline. You can also use <h2>, <h3>, and <h4> for headlines of decreasing size and importance.

- ◆ <p> defines a paragraph section; this tag creates a line break before and after the content inside.

- ◆ Anything between <a> tags is a link. For example, <a href="http://www.couldbestudios.com">couldbe studios</a> creates a hyperlink to the CouldBe Studios Web site.

For more information on basic HTML, check out www.w3schools.com/html/html_primary.asp.

Figure 10.1 Kubrick's default header.

Figure 10.2 Click the Custom Header link in the sidebar to make changes to the default header.

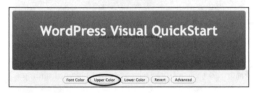

Figure 10.3 Customization options for the default theme's header.

The default WordPress theme, Kubrick, has a header with a nice blue gradient, or graduated color, background that displays the site's title and description (**Figure 10.1**). The default theme is designed to make this header easy to modify.

To modify the default theme's header:

1. In the left sidebar, choose Appearance > Custom Header (**Figure 10.2**).

   A preview will be displayed, with buttons for the various customizable elements. You can change the font color, the color of the upper gradient, and the color of the lower gradient.

2. Click Upper Color to begin (**Figure 10.3**).

continues on next page

CHANGING A THEME'S APPEARANCE

3. In the color picker that appears, click on the color you wish to use for the top of the gradient fill, and then click Close Color Picker (**Figure 10.4**).

The header will disappear for a moment and then reappear, displaying the new color you've chosen at the top of the background area.

4. To change the lower background color, click Lower Color and repeat step 3. To make the background a solid color, choose the same color for both the top and the bottom of the gradient.

5. To change the color of the font, click Font Color and repeat step 3.

6. Click Update Header when you are done making changes, and the resulting preview matches what you want to see (**Figure 10.5**).

There may be slight differences between the preview and what is actually displayed on your site—for example, the blog name and tagline may be out of alignment, or the gradient may not display accurately— so it's a good idea to take a look at your site after you make changes.

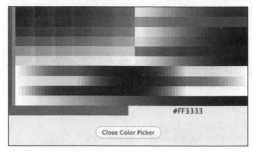

Figure 10.4 Use the color picker to choose the colors you want for the header background.

Figure 10.5 Click Update Header to save your changes.

✔ Tips

- It's always a good idea to back up your theme files before making any changes to them.

- If you don't like your changes, you can always click Revert to go back to the original color scheme.

- Chapter 11, "DIY Theme Building," explores how themes are structured and what the various template files do, so if this chapter whets your theme-modifying appetite, make sure you read on!

- If you are trying to get support for modifying an existing theme, often the best place to find ways to make commonly requested changes is the theme author's site. Check the style.css file in the theme, which you can access by clicking Appearance > Editor in your WordPress admin area. Often a URL to the author's site is contained in the metadata at the top of the file (**Figure 10.6**).

```
/*
Theme Name: WordPress Default
Theme URI: http://wordpress.org/
Description: The default WordPress theme based on the famous <a href="http://binarybonsai.com/kubrick/">Kubrick</a>.
Version: 1.6
Author: Michael Heilemann
Author URI: http://binarybonsai.com/
Tags: blue, custom header, fixed width, two columns, widgets
```

Figure 10.6 The metadata at the top of the style.css file for the WordPress default theme. You can usually find the theme author's URL here.

Making Your Theme Widget-ready

Widgets were introduced with the release of WordPress 2.2, and theme builders have been eagerly taking advantage of them ever since. You can learn more about widgets and what they can do in Chapter 9, "Widgets and Plug-ins." If the theme you are using was written before WordPress began using widgets or doesn't include support for them, you can add that support by modifying the theme files.

Although the process is fairly simple, you should have at least a basic understanding of PHP and HTML before attempting this task.

To widgetize your theme:

1. Choose Appearance > Editor in the left sidebar to open the Edit Themes page.

2. Click Sidebar (sidebar.php) in the list of template files on the right (**Figure 10.7**). The Sidebar template file will open in the editing window.

   The actual structure of this file will vary from theme to theme, so we will use the same basic example that is found at the WordPress Codex (codex.wordpress.org/ Widgetizing_Themes).

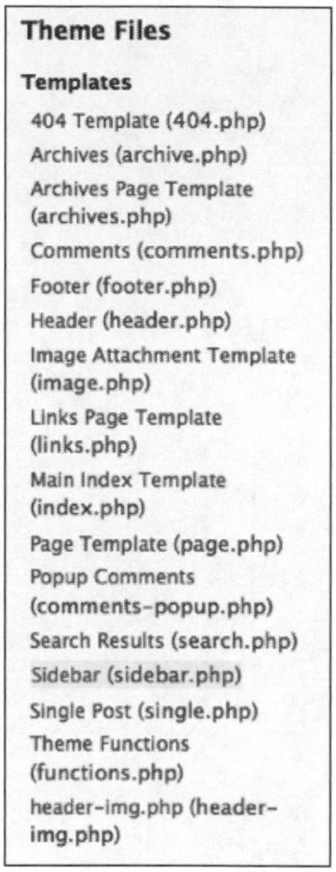

Theme Files

Templates

404 Template (404.php)

Archives (archive.php)

Archives Page Template (archives.php)

Comments (comments.php)

Footer (footer.php)

Header (header.php)

Image Attachment Template (image.php)

Links Page Template (links.php)

Main Index Template (index.php)

Page Template (page.php)

Popup Comments (comments-popup.php)

Search Results (search.php)

Sidebar (sidebar.php)

Single Post (single.php)

Theme Functions (functions.php)

header-img.php (header-img.php)

Figure 10.7 A list of template files in the theme editor. All the files that make up the theme can be edited here. Click a filename to open it in the editing window.

Although not a requirement, it is most common for themes to mark up the sidebar as an unordered list (shortened in the markup to <ul>) like the one shown here:

```
<ul id="sidebar">
     <li id="about">
       <h2>About</h2>
       <p>This is my blog.</p>
     </li>
     <li id="links">
       <h2>Links</h2>
  <ul>
    <li>
      <a href="http://example.
      → com">Example</a>
    </li>
  </ul>
     </li>
</ul>
```

3. To add widget support to the sidebar, you will need to add two lines of code to the list.

First, you need to have your template look for the function that handles widgets. In PHP the function is called Dynamic Sidebar (dynamic_sidebar), and you activate it by inserting some code into your unordered list. To do this, add the following code just inside the main <ul> tag for the sidebar:

```
<?php if(!function_exists
→ ('dynamic_sidebar') ||
→ !dynamic_sidebar() ) : ?>
```

continues on next page

4. Next, you must instruct the template to stop looking for the Dynamic Sidebar so that WordPress doesn't just loop endlessly through the function, displaying the same widgets over and over. Add the following code just before the closing </ul> tag for the sidebar:

```
<?php endif; ?>
```

The sidebar list should now look something like this:

```
<ul id="sidebar">
<?php if( !function_exists
→ ('dynamic_sidebar')        ||
→ !dynamic_sidebar() ) : ?>
      <li id="about">
        <h2>About</h2>
        <p>This is my blog.</p>
      </li>
      <li id="links">
        <h2>Links</h2>
      <ul>
      <li>
        <a href="http://example.com">
        → Example</a>
      </li>
      </ul>
      </li>
<?php endif; ?>
</ul>
```

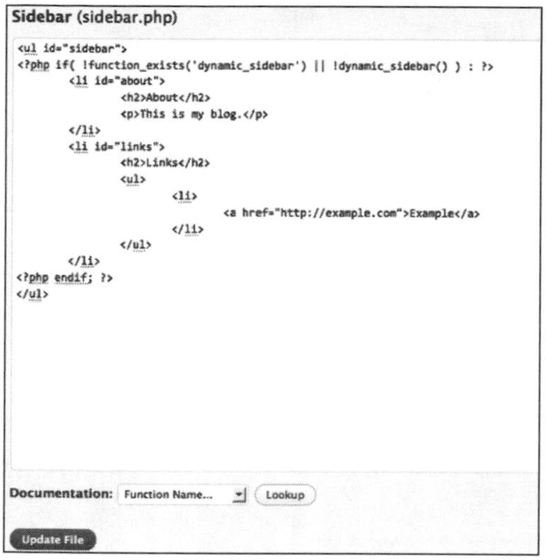

```
Sidebar (sidebar.php)

<ul id="sidebar">
<?php if( !function_exists('dynamic_sidebar') || !dynamic_sidebar() ) : ?>
        <li id="about">
                <h2>About</h2>
                <p>This is my blog.</p>
        </li>
        <li id="links">
                <h2>Links</h2>
                <ul>
                        <li>
                                <a href="http://example.com">Example</a>
                        </li>
                </ul>
        </li>
<?php endif; ?>
</ul>
```

Documentation: Function Name... ▾ (Lookup)

(Update File)

Figure 10.8 Update the sidebar.php file with your customizations.

5. Click Update File to save the changes you have made to sidebar.php (**Figure 10.8**).

6. Now that you have added the code to your sidebar that will check for widgets, you need to tell your theme how to use widgets. To do this, you will need to add a function. Click Theme Functions (functions.php) in the list of template files on the right.

7. To the functions.php file, add the following code:

```
<?php if ( function_
exists('register_sidebar') )
→ register_sidebar(); ?>
```

8. Click Update File to save the changes to functions.php. Your theme now supports widgets in the sidebar.

9. Choose Appearance > Widgets in the left sidebar menu to access the widget system. Chapter 9 provides a detailed walkthrough of installing and managing widgets.

✔ Tip

■ You can find more information about adding widget capability to themes at http://codex.wordpress.org/Widgetizing_Themes.

Customizing Your Theme with CSS

If you know CSS, you can make some major changes to the look and feel of your theme without touching the underlying structure. You'll use style sheets to change text colors, background color, and font styles.

A style sheet is a CSS file that tells your browser how to display the site. Almost all WordPress themes use a style sheet called style.css for the main CSS (**Figure 10.9**). Some themes include additional style sheets, which you will be able to see in the list of files in the theme editor.

When you open the Edit Themes page in your WordPress admin section, the first template file that will display is your current theme's style sheet. If you need to open the style sheet after you've clicked on another template file, you can always find it at the bottom of the list of theme files in the Edit Themes sidebar.

It is important to note that style.css always starts with a comment that contains a block of metadata about the theme (**Figure 10.10**). *Do not* delete this data! WordPress uses the metadata to provide information and identification for the theme in the admin panel (**Figure 10.11**). If you're building a theme from scratch, you can put your own information in this comment section so that anyone viewing your CSS file will know who created it.

Theme Files

Templates

404 Template (404.php)
Archives (archive.php)
Archives Page Template (archives.php)
Attachment Template (attachment.php)
Comments (comments.php)
Footer (footer.php)
Header (header.php)
Image Attachment Template (image.php)
Links Page Template (links.php)
Main Index Template (index.php)
Page Template (page.php)
Popup Comments (comments–popup.php)
Search Form (searchform.php)
Search Results (search.php)
Sidebar (sidebar.php)
Single Post (single.php)
Theme Functions (functions.php)
header–img.php (header–img.php)

Styles

RTL Stylesheet (rtl.css)
Stylesheet (style.css)

Figure 10.9 A list of style sheets in the sidebar of the theme editor.

```
Version: 1.6
Author: Michael Heilemann
Author URI: http://binarybonsai.com/
Tags: blue, custom header, fixed width, two columns, widgets

        Kubrick v1.5
        http://binarybonsai.com/kubrick/

        This theme was designed and built by Michael Heilemann,
        whose blog you will find at http://binarybonsai.com/

        The CSS, XHTML and design is released under GPL:
        http://www.opensource.org/licenses/gpl-license.php
```

Figure 10.10 The theme metadata, which is used to identify the theme in the WordPress admin.

Current Theme

WordPress Default 1.6 by Michael Heilemann

The default WordPress theme based on the famous Kubrick.

All of this theme's files are located in /themes/default .

Tags: blue, custom header, fixed width, two columns, widgets

Figure 10.11 A theme in the WordPress admin area, with the metadata providing information such as author and tags.

```
body {
        font-size: 62.5%; /* Resets 1em to 10px */
        font-family: 'Lucida Grande', Verdana, Arial, Sans-Serif;
        background: #d5d6d7 url('images/kubrickbgcolor.jpg');
        color: #333;
        text-align: center;
        }
```

Figure 10.12 The style.css entry for text color.

What Is CSS?

Your CSS (Cascading Style Sheets) file controls how your site looks to your visitors. It lets you make changes to the look of your site without touching the underlying XHTML, which means you can make significant tweaks to your entire site by modifying only the CSS file. For an idea of how much a site can change using CSS alone, check out CSS Zen Garden (www. csszengarden.com).

CSS works by specifying sections of the HTML (called *selectors*) and telling the browser how to display them. The format for a CSS file is slightly different from HTML, though the selectors are the same in both. For example, here is a paragraph in HTML:

```
<p>I am a paragraph.</p>
```

To modify the paragraph selector to display with a 10pixel margin on all sides using CSS, you would type this:

```
p {
margin:10px;
}
```

To change text color with CSS:

1. Choose a color scheme for your site's text. You can choose colors for any text on your site, but important ones are main text, links, headers, and footers.

2. Look at the style.css file in the theme editor and find the entry for the main text color, simply called `color` (**Figure 10.12**).

3. CSS colors are entered in hexadecimal format; a good online color picking resource is available at http://www. febooti.com/products/iezoom/online-help/online-color-chart-picker.html. Enter the hexadecimal color for your main text, starting with a hash mark. It will look something like this:
   `color:#000000;`

4. Find the other text you'd like to color and repeat step 3.

5. Click Update File to save your changes.

✔ Tip

■ There are many online resources for choosing color schemes. Two that we like are Adobe's kuler (http://kuler.adobe.com) and COLOURLovers (www.colourlovers.com).

CUSTOMIZING YOUR THEME WITH CSS

To change the background color with CSS:

1. Choose a background color that you would like to use.

2. In the style.css file, find the body section and look for the word background (**Figure 10.13**).

3. Replace the existing background color with the hexadecimal color of your choice.

4. Click Update File to save your changes.

Since CSS doesn't actually contain font files, it's best to choose a Web-compatible font, or one that is commonly found on Windows or Mac computers. If the font you want to use is platform specific or may not be available to all visitors to your site, you can also choose an alternate font that will harmonize with your site's look and feel.

✔ Tip

■ A great resource for finding and previewing Web-compatible fonts is Typetester (www.typetester.org/).

To change font style with CSS:

1. In the style.css file, find the body section and locate the line that begins with font-family (**Figure 10.14**).

2. Enter your font choice, along with an alternate option if you wish, and note whether the font is serif or sans-serif. Separate each option with a comma, like this:

   font-family: Georgia,
   → 'Times New Roman', serif;

3. Click Update File to save your changes.

```
background: #d5d6d7 url('images/kubrickbgcolor.jpg');
```

Figure 10.13 The style.css entry for background color.

```
font-family: 'Lucida Grande', Verdana, Arial, Sans-Serif;
```

Figure 10.14 The font-family section of style.css.

Figure 10.15 A favicon in the Firefox address bar

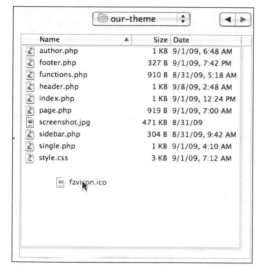

Figure 10.16 Upload your favicon to the main folder of your current theme.

Working with Favicons

A favicon, short for favorites icon, is a tiny 16-by-16-pixel graphic that appears next to a site's URL and title in the title bar on most browsers (**Figure 10.15**). A favicon is often used for visual identification in a browser's bookmarks as well as in the address bar and on tabs.

To add a favicon to your site:

1. Using a graphics program such as GIMP (www.gimp.org), create a 16-by-16-pixel image. You can also use an online favicon generator such as favikon (http://favikon.com/).

2. Save the file as an ICO file with the name favicon.ico.

3. Upload the favicon.ico file to your current theme's main folder (**Figure 10.16**).

4. In the theme editor, open the header.php file.

continues on next page

5. Find the line that begins with
`<link rel="shortcut icon"` and ends
with `/favicon.ico" />`. Overwrite it or
add the following code below the `<head>`
HTML tag (**Figure 10.17**):

```
<link rel="shortcut icon" href=
→ "<?php bloginfo('template_
→ directory'); ?>/favicon.ico" />
```

6. Click Update File to save your changes.
Your new favicon will now display next to
your URL in most browsers.

Header (header.php)

```
<!DOCTYPE html PUBLIC "-//W3C//DTD XHTML 1.0 Transitional//EN"
    "http://www.w3.org/TR/xhtml1/DTD/xhtml1-transitional.dtd">

<html xmlns="http://www.w3.org/1999/xhtml" xml:lang="en" lang="en">
<head>
    <meta http-equiv="Content-Type" content="text/html; charset=utf-8"/>
    <meta name="description" content="<?php bloginfo('description'); ?>"/>
    <title><?php bloginfo('name'); ?> <?php wp_title(); ?></title>

<link rel="shortcut icon" href="<?php bloginfo('template_directory'); ?>/favicon.ico" />
```

Figure 10.17 Enter the favicon code in your header.php file.

Advanced Theme Development

In this chapter, we will help you to design and build a simple theme from scratch. Theme building in WordPress requires a strong knowledge of Web design, HTML/XHTML, CSS, and PHP. In other words, novice users need not apply! For designers and developers, however, building your own theme offers unparalleled flexibility and power, especially when compared to using or modifying a prebuilt theme.

WordPress has two themes installed by default, and both are excellent examples of different approaches to theme building. It's a good idea to examine those themes to get an idea of layout and structure before digging into your own.

Anatomy of a Theme

Your theme may appear as one cohesive whole, but many different pieces go into each page of a site (**Figure 11.1**). Themes generally are made up of three types of files: style sheets, template files, and optionally a function file. Most themes also include some background images, and if the theme will be distributed, a thumbnail screen shot image.

Your site will function with only a style sheet named style.css and an index.php template file, but to create a full-featured theme you will need to set up several more template files. All of these files go in the theme's directory.

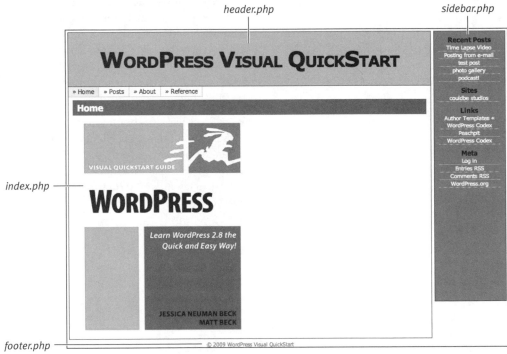

Figure 11.1 The front page of our site is composed of several files: header.php (1), index.php (2), sidebar.php (3), and footer.php (4).

If you do not include certain files (such as comments.php), WordPress will pull the default versions into your site. However, it's a good idea to generate your own versions of those files, as the defaults will most likely not match your site very well.

In building your theme, we recommend that you use your text editor to edit theme files. Once you have a basic theme working, it's possible to install it on your site and make changes using the built-in theme editor in WordPress. However, a traditional text editor will work better considering the amount of code you are going to be writing.

✔ Tip

- Looking for the template files for your theme? In your WordPress install directory, themes are located in the subdirectories of /wp-content/themes/. Your custom theme would, for example, be located in /wp-content/themes/name-of-theme.

Theme-Building Shortcuts: Frameworks and Blueprints

Frameworks and blueprints are great ways to save time when building a new theme, since the site's basic structure is built right in. Numerous frameworks are available, and many of them are created just for WordPress.

One of the most popular theme frameworks is Sandbox, a minimalist, unstyled WordPress theme developed by Scott Allan Wallick and Andy Skelton. Since it is licensed under the GNU General Public License, you can modify it to your heart's content and publish it as your own, provided that you leave the original theme credit intact. Sandbox is a fully functioning theme with several different variations as well as built-in widget support and microformatting. It's a great starting point for developing a new theme. You can download Sandbox or learn more about it at www.plaintxt.org/themes/sandbox/.

Blueprint is a CSS framework that gives you a head start on common styling like typography, column widths, and cross-browser compatibility. Sure, you could manually add all that to each theme you build—but with Blueprint, you don't have to! Blueprint is available at www.blueprintcss.org/ and you can obtain a WordPress-specific version at www.fireandknowledge.org/blueprint/.

ANATOMY OF A THEME

Building a Theme from Scratch

If you've always wanted to build your own theme, this is the section for you! Theme building is by far too broad a topic to cover completely here, but we can give you the basic tools you will need to get started.

✔ Tips

- To get a better grasp of how all these code snippets go together, download the complete working example theme from our site at http://Wordpress28vqs.com/our-theme.zip. It's the same theme used on the site and discussed in this book.

- For more information on themes and how to build them, check out Theme Development on the WordPress Codex: http://codex.wordpress.org/Theme_Development.

To create a basic blank theme:

1. Using your FTP client, create a new directory for your theme in your WordPress site's /wp-content/themes directory (**Figure 11.2**). Name this directory after your new theme—/wp-content/themes/our-theme, for example.

2. To set up this theme, we're going to create four template pages and one style sheet. Create a new file called index.php and upload it to the directory you just created.

3. Repeat the process to create header.php, sidebar.php, footer.php, and style.css files, and upload them to the same place (**Figure 11.3**).

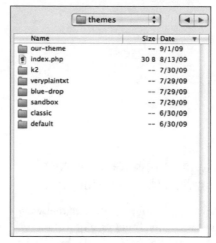

Figure 11.2 The wp-content/themes directory contains subdirectories for each theme you have installed.

Figure 11.3 A basic theme could consist of just style.css and index.php and still function correctly.

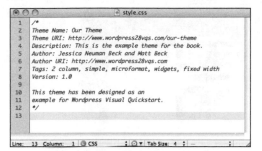

Figure 11.4 The style.css file holds some important settings in a required comment block.

4. Using your favorite text editor such as TextMate for the Mac or TextPad on Windows, open your style.css file and add the following required comment section at the top (**Figure 11.4**):

/*

Theme Name: Our Theme

Theme URI: http://www.wordpress28vqs

→ .com/our-theme

Description: This is the example

→ theme for the book.

Author: Jessica Neuman Beck and

→ Matt Beck

Author URI: http://www.

→ wordpress28vqs.com

Tags: 2 column, simple, microformat,

→ widgets, fixed width

Version: 1.0

This theme has been designed as

→ an example for WordPress Visual

→ QuickStart.

*/

You will notice that the comment section begins and ends with /* and */. Everything between those symbols is considered a comment and is ignored by browsers looking for style information.

This comment contains several variables followed by a colon and a value. The required variables are Theme Name, Theme URI, Description, Author, and Author URI. The optional variables are Tags, Template, and Version. If you do not wish to use one of the optional variables, just leave it out completely.

continues on next page

5. After listing the variables in the comment block, enter any additional text you'd like to include, such as licensing information.

For example, in the previous code, the line This theme has been designed as an example for WordPress Visual QuickStart is the type of additional text you might enter in this section. Just make sure you place the text after the required variables and before the final */ symbol.

6. Save and close your style.css file and upload it to your theme's directory.

The data in the comment block, and a screen shot if you have provided one (see the following tip for instructions on including a screen shot), will be displayed in the WordPress back-end in the Themes subpanel (**Figure 11.5**). You can access the subpanel by logging in to your admin area and clicking Appearance.

7. Open the header.php file in your text editor. This is the file that will control the information your visitors will see at the top of your Web site; it will also contain meta-information that is not displayed on your site but that conveys important information to browsers (such as where to find other template files).

8. Add a document type (DOCTYPE) to your header.php file. This tells the browser how to interpret the XHTML code. For our theme, we used the following:

```
<!DOCTYPE html PUBLIC "-//W3C//
→ DTD XHTML 1.0 Transitional//EN"
→ "http://www.w3.org/TR/xhtml1/DTD/
→ xhtml1-transitional.dtd">
```

You can find more information on doc-types at the W3C Web site (www.w3.org/QA/Tips/Doctype).

Our Theme 1.0 by Jessica Neuman Beck **and Matt Beck**

This is the example theme for the book.

Activate | Preview | Delete

All of this theme's files are located in /themes /our-theme .

Tags: 2 column, simple, microformat, widgets, fixed width

Figure 11.5 Information from style.css is displayed in the Themes subpanel.

9. After the DOCTYPE declaration, add your theme's meta-information (**Figure 11.6**). This information goes between <head> </head> tags, which tells the browser that the information is to be processed before the main body of the Web site (which comes next).

Here are some metatags you may want to add to your header.php file:

```
<meta http-equiv="Content-Type"
→ content="text/html; charset=
→ utf-8"/>
```

This sets the content type for your site and ensures that the browser will interpret symbols and text correctly.

```
<meta name="description" content=
→ "<?php bloginfo('description');
→ ?>"/>
```

continues on next page

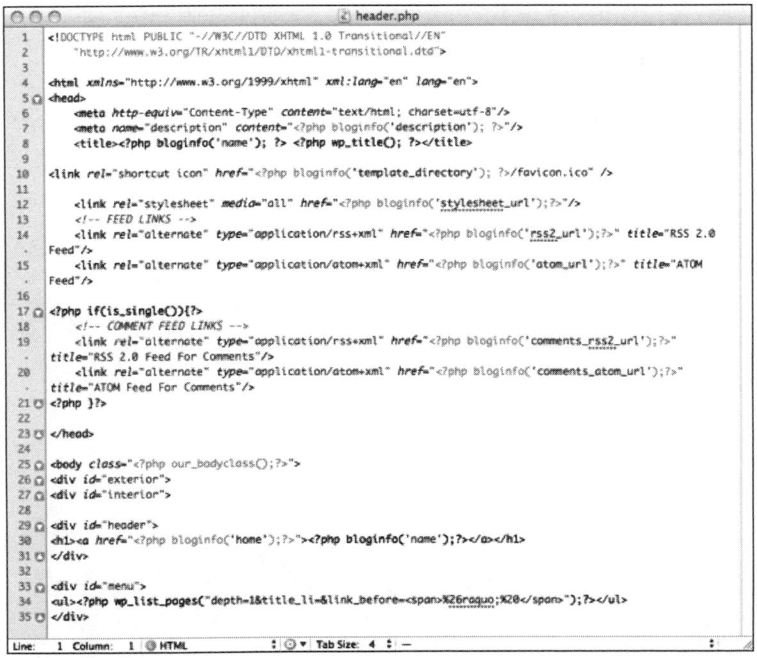

```
header.php
1   <!DOCTYPE html PUBLIC "-//W3C//DTD XHTML 1.0 Transitional//EN"
2      "http://www.w3.org/TR/xhtml1/DTD/xhtml1-transitional.dtd">
3
4   <html xmlns="http://www.w3.org/1999/xhtml" xml:lang="en" lang="en">
5   <head>
6       <meta http-equiv="Content-Type" content="text/html; charset=utf-8"/>
7       <meta name="description" content="<?php bloginfo('description'); ?>"/>
8       <title><?php bloginfo('name'); ?> <?php wp_title(); ?></title>
9
10  <link rel="shortcut icon" href="<?php bloginfo('template_directory'); ?>/favicon.ico" />
11
12      <link rel="stylesheet" media="all" href="<?php bloginfo('stylesheet_url');?>"/>
13      <!-- FEED LINKS -->
14      <link rel="alternate" type="application/rss+xml" href="<?php bloginfo('rss2_url');?>" title="RSS 2.0
.   Feed"/>
15      <link rel="alternate" type="application/atom+xml" href="<?php bloginfo('atom_url');?>" title="ATOM
.   Feed"/>
16
17  <?php if(is_single()){?>
18      <!-- COMMENT FEED LINKS -->
19      <link rel="alternate" type="application/rss+xml" href="<?php bloginfo('comments_rss2_url');?>"
.   title="RSS 2.0 Feed For Comments"/>
20      <link rel="alternate" type="application/atom+xml" href="<?php bloginfo('comments_atom_url');?>"
.   title="ATOM Feed For Comments"/>
21  <?php }?>
22
23  </head>
24
25  <body class="<?php our_bodyclass();?>">
26  <div id="exterior">
27  <div id="interior">
28
29  <div id="header">
30  <h1><a href="<?php bloginfo('home');?>"><?php bloginfo('name');?></a></h1>
31  </div>
32
33  <div id="menu">
34  <ul><?php wp_list_pages("depth=1&title_li=&link_before=<span>%26raquo;%20</span>");?></ul>
35  </div>

Line:   1   Column:   1   HTML                    Tab Size:  4
```

Figure 11.6 The header.php file contains some important information for browsers.

This is the description for your site. Using the WordPress shortcode `bloginfo('description')` pulls the description directly from the Settings section of your WordPress admin area.

```
<title><?php bloginfo('name');
→ ?> <?php wp_title();
→ ?></title>
```

The `<title>` tag also uses shortcode to pull in the title of your site from the Settings section of your WordPress admin area. This title displays on the top of your browser window.

```
<link rel="stylesheet" media=
→ "all" href="<?php bloginfo
→ ('stylesheet_url');?>"/>
```

This tag tells the browser where to find the style sheet. It's very important to include it!

10. After the final closing `</head>` tag, add opening `<html>` and `<body>` tags (we will close these tags in the footer.php file). Now you can add the code that will display in the header of your site, such as the site's name. Here's an example:

```
<div id="header">
<h1><a href="<?php bloginfo
→ ('home');?>"><?php bloginfo
→ ('name');?></a></h1>
</div>
```

11. Save your header.php file and upload it to your theme's directory.

12. Open the index.php file and add the XHTML structure for the main portion of your site, including the WordPress Loop (described later in this chapter, in the section "Using the Loop") (**Figure 11.7**). The index.php file provides the primary structure for the body of your site. Make sure you include the shortcode that will pull in the header, sidebar, and footer files.

13. Save and close your index.php file and upload it to your template directory.

continues on next page

```php
<?php get_header();?>

<div id="content">

<!--START THE LOOP-->
<?php if ( have_posts() ) : while ( have_posts() ) : the_post(); ?>

<div class="entry">
    <h2 class="entry-title"><a href="<?php the_permalink(); ?>"><?php the_title(); ?></a></h2>
    <div class="entry-body">
        <?php the_content(); ?>
        <div class="metadata">
            <span class="author">By <?php the_author_posts_link(); ?><span><br/>
            <span class="date"><?php the_time('F jS, Y'); ?></span><br/>
            <span class="categories">Categories <?php the_category(' &raquo; '); ?></span><br/>
            <?php
            $taglist = get_the_tags();
            if ($taglist) {
                echo "<span class=\"tags\">Tags ";
                $lasttag=end($taglist);
                foreach($taglist as $val) {
                    echo "<a href=\"".get_tag_link($val->term_id)."\" rel=\"tag\">".$val->name."</a>";
                    if($val != $lasttag){echo ", ";}
                }
                echo "</span>";
            }
            ?>
        </div>
    </div>
</div>

<!--END THE LOOP-->
```

Figure 11.7 Include the WordPress Loop as well as the shortcode to pull in your header, sidebar, and footer files in your index.php file.

14. Open your sidebar.php file and add any information you want to display in your sidebar. If you want to include support for widgets in your sidebar, check out the "To widgetize your theme" task in Chapter 10.

15. Save and close your sidebar.php file and upload it to your theme directory.

16. Open the footer.php file and enter the information you want to appear in your site's footer. Often this is copyright and design information, as in this example:

```
<cite>&copy; <?php echo date('Y');
→ ?> <a href="<?php bloginfo
→ ('url');?>"><?php bloginfo
→ ('name');?></a></cite>
```

17. At the end of your footer file, close the <body> and <html> tags you opened in the header.php file (**Figure 11.8**). Make sure the last lines of your footer.php file include this code:

```
</body>
</html>
```

18. Save and close your footer.php file and upload it to your theme directory.

At this point, you have a basic skeleton of a WordPress site. Next you'll need to add CSS styling and design elements to style.css and flesh out your site with a navigation menu, a sidebar, and any other elements you want to include.

✔ Tips

■ WordPress will use the default versions of any templates you leave out, so if, for example, your theme doesn't include a comment.php file, WordPress will handle comments using the wp-comments.php file located in the core WordPress directory.

■ A detailed walkthrough demonstrating how to build a theme with file-by-file breakdowns and full code samples is available on our site at http://wordpress28vqs.com/reference/theme-building.

■ You can include an image of your finished theme to display in the WordPress Themes admin area by uploading a 300 by 225-pixel JPEG or PNG file called "screenshot" to your theme's directory.

```
footer.php
1  <div id="footer">
2  <cite>&copy; <?php echo date('Y');?> <a href="<?php bloginfo('url');?>"><?php
   bloginfo('name');?></a></cite>
3  </div>
4
5  </div><!--/exterior-->
6
7  </body>
8  </html>
```

Figure 11.8 Close the <body> and <html> tags in your footer.php file.

Working with Template Files

Template files are where all of the magic happens in your theme. These files pull data from your site's database and generate the HTML that will be displayed on your site.

WordPress typically generates dynamic content by using two different types of templates:

◆ Those that generate a specific display—such as single.php, which is used to display a single blog post display—are essentially a replacement for the index.php file.

◆ Those that are included in other templates—such as header.php, sidebar.php, and footer.php—need to be placed in another template in order to function, like a piece of a jigsaw puzzle.

You can also create your own templates when building a theme, even if they are not automatically recognized in the WordPress template hierarchy. Instead of using a WordPress template tag to include the file, you can use the PHP `include()` function with the `TEMPLATEPATH` variable to do so:

```
<?php include (TEMPLATEPATH .
→ '/templatename.php'); ?>
```

✔ Tips

■ You can find more information about the WordPress template files at http://wordpress28vqs.com/reference/wordpress-templates/.

■ See "Template Hierarchy" later in the chapter to understand which templates are displayed in which order.

WordPress Template Files

While you can create a functional site using only the style.css and index.php files, WordPress gives you the option of utilizing many different templates. The following is a list of templates automatically recognized by WordPress. Use some of them in your next theme!

◆ Page Not Found Template (404.php)

◆ Archive Template (archive.php)

◆ Archive Index Template (archives.php)

◆ Comments Template (comments.php)

◆ Footer Template (footer.php)

◆ Header Template (header.php)

◆ Links (links.php)

◆ Main Template (index.php)

◆ Page Template (page.php)

◆ Popup Comments Template (comments-popup.php)

◆ Post Template (single.php)

◆ Search Form (searchform.php)

◆ Search Template (search.php)

◆ Sidebar Template (sidebar.php)

◆ User Defined Templates (templatename.php)

Template hierarchy

Most of the available WordPress templates are not mandatory, and WordPress provides a hierarchy to show the order of templates it looks for when displaying content.

For example, if your theme includes a home.php template, WordPress will use that template to display content when a viewer navigates to your home page. But if the home.php template isn't included in your theme, WordPress will display the content using the index.php template instead. A more complicated example is something like tag display—if you have a tag.php file, WordPress will use that file when someone clicks on one of your tags. If you don't have a tag.php file, WordPress will use the archive.php file to display your tagged posts. If you don't have an archive.php file either, WordPress will use the index.php template to display the content.

You will notice that index.php is the baseline that all the displays default to, so take care when crafting it.

Home Page display

1. home.php
2. index.php

Single Post display

1. single.php
2. index.php

Page display

1. pagetemplate.php
2. page.php
3. index.php

Category display

1. category-id.php (if the category's ID is 6, WordPress will look for category-6.php)
2. category.php

3. archive.php

4. index.php

Tag display

1. tag-slug.php (if the tag's slug is sometag, WordPress will look for tag-sometag.php)

2. tag.php

3. archive.php

4. index.php

Author display

1. author.php

2. archive.php

3. index.php

Date display

1. date.php

2. archive.php

3. index.php

Search Result display

1. search.php

2. index.php

404 (Not Found) display

1. 404.php

2. index.php

Attachment display

1. image.php, video.php, audio.php, application.php, or any other first part of the MIME type

2. attachment.php

3. single.php

4. index.php

Archive Index display

1. archives.php

2. index.php

WORKING WITH TEMPLATE FILES

Modifying Templates

Making site-wide changes is easy when you use templates. A change made to your header.php file, for example, will affect every page on your site.

To add a background graphic to your theme using CSS:

1. Find your image file and save it to the exact dimensions you want to display on your site.

   If your site has a background color other than white and your image has areas that are meant to be transparent, either modify your image to use the same background color as your site (using Photoshop or a similar graphics program) or save it as a GIF or a PNG with a transparent background.

2. Upload your image file to your theme directory using FTP.

3. Open your stylesheet.css file. You will see a section called body that lets you choose the attributes for the main body of your site. In our example, the body style includes a color and a font size as well as a background. To add a background image, enter the following code:

   ```
   background: url('myimage.jpg')
   → top left no-repeat;
   ```

```
body{
    background:url('image.jpg') top left no-repeat;
    color:#111;
    font-size:13px;
    }
```

Figure 11.9 This is what the body section of the style sheet will look like if you want to add an image to the top left of your site.

4. Replace *myimage.jpg* with your image name and extension (**Figure 11.9**).

This tells your browser to display the linked image in the background of the body of your site. The `top left no-repeat` command tells the browser to display the image on the top-left side of your site, and only show it once. You can change these options to display your image the way you want (for example, bottom right or top center), and if you want your image to repeat over the entirety of your site, simply change `no-repeat` to `repeat`.

5. Save and close the style.css file.

To add graphics to a template file:

1. To add a logo or other image to a template file, save the image to your theme folder via FTP. Make sure the image is saved to the exact dimensions you want to display.

2. Open the template file you want to modify (for this example, we're adding a logo to the header.php file).

3. Find the place in the file where you want to add the image. In this case, since we're adding a logo, we'll be replacing the `<?php bloginfo('name');?>` tag with the tag for our image (**Figure 11.10**).

continues on next page

```
<div id="header">
<h1><a href="<?php bloginfo('home');?>"><?php bloginfo('name');?></a></h1>
</div>
```

Figure 11.10 In the header.php file, find the `<?php bloginfo('name');?>` tag to prepare to replace with the image tag.

MODIFYING TEMPLATES

4. Enter the tag to display your image.

5. To generate a URL to the theme directory, use the `template_url` parameter of the `bloginfo` template tag in front of the image filename like so:

```
<img src="<?php    bloginfo
→ ('template_url'); ?>/filename.
→ jpg"/>
```

Once you're done, it will look something like this:

```
<div id="header">
<h1><a href="<?php bloginfo
→ ('home');?>"> <img src="<?php
→ bloginfo('template_url');
→ ?>/ logo.jpg"/></a></h1>
</div>
```

6. Save your header.php file and close it.

To add menu navigation to your theme:

1. In your text editor, open the theme template to which you wish to add a menu (typically header.php).

2. Add the `wp_list_pages` template tag to generate a list of links to your WordPress pages (**Figure 11.11**).

```
<div id="menu">
<ul><?php wp_list_pages("depth=1&title_li=&link_before=<span>%26raquo;%20</span>");?></ul>
</div>
```

Figure 11.11 These tabs are links in an unordered list, generated by `wp_list_pages`.

In this example, we're specifying that we want only top-level (parent) pages to show on the navigation menu by putting "depth=1" in parentheses. The rest of the code tells the browser to display each navigation link in a `<span>` preceded with a >> symbol:

```
<div id="menu">
<ul>
<?php wp_list_pages("depth=
→ 1&title_li=&link_before=
→ <span>%26raquo;%20</span>");
?>
</ul>
</div>
```

✔ Tip

- Our example adds only top-level pages from the taxonomy of your site. To include subpages in your menu, adjust the `depth` parameter in the function call. For example, if you want to show parent pages and second-level child pages, change the code to read `depth=2`.

Working with Template Tags

Template tags are PHP functions that pull information from the database for your WordPress site and display it or make it available for you to manipulate with PHP when used in your theme templates.

Many of the template tags accept parameters, or modifiers that let you manipulate the information that is pulled from the database and/or change what is output by the function. The parameters accepted (if any) vary from tag to tag.

There are two ways that template tags accept parameters: either by accepting standard PHP function parameters (strings, arrays, and the like) or with a query-string-style parameter.

To use a template tag with standard PHP parameters:

1. Open your header.php file in a text editor or in the Edit Themes section of your WordPress admin.

2. Find the `bloginfo` tag.

3. Refer to the list of available parameters for the `bloginfo` tag on the WordPress Codex at http://codex.wordpress.org/Template_Tags/bloginfo to see a full list of options.

   The `bloginfo` tag can accept a single string as a parameter—for example, `<?php bloginfo('description'); ?>`—which will output the description of your site as specified in the General Settings section of your admin screen.

4. Enter your chosen parameter in parentheses and single quotes after `bloginfo`.

5. Save and close your header.php file.

To use a template tag with a query-string-style parameter:

1. Open your header.php file in a text editor or the Edit Themes section of your WordPress admin area.

2. Locate the `wp_list_pages` template tag, which is part of your navigation list. It will look something like this:

   ```
   <?php wp_list_pages('sort_column=
   → menu_order&depth=2'); ?>
   ```

3. Refer to the WordPress Codex for an available list of parameters for the `wp_list_pages` tag at http://codex.wordpress.org/Template_Tags/wp_list_pages. The configuration in the previous example will generate a list of pages sorted by the menu order, including sub-pages of the top-level pages.

4. Enter the parameters you'd like to include, using parentheses and single quotes, with each section of the query string separated by the ampersand (&) symbol.

5. Save and close your header.php file.

✔ Tips

■ Many of the template tags that output content directly to the page in HTML format have a corresponding tag that provides that data to PHP instead. By convention, most of these are prefixed with `get_`, such as `get_bloginfo()`, which returns the same dynamic data as `bloginfo()` but returns the value instead of displaying it. This allows you to use PHP to manipulate the output for advanced uses.

■ A detailed listing of the available template tags can be found on the WordPress Codex at http://codex.wordpress.org/Template_Tags.

Include tags

Include tags are template tags that pull one WordPress template into another template. A single page in a WordPress site may be made up of several includes, such as an index page comprised of header.php, sidebar.php, and footer.php, in addition to the index.php template.

When a template file calls for an include tag that isn't part of a theme, it will use the default template in the order defined by the template hierarchy. A good example of this is a single post page (single.php) that includes a comment.php section that isn't part of the theme (**Figure 11.12**). The effect is seamless; most viewers would have no idea they were looking at a patchwork of templates.

To use include tags:

1. In your text editor, open the parent template in which you wish to include a subtemplate.

2. Add the include tag you wish to use, such as the following:

   ```
   <div id="comments">
   <?php comments_template(); ?>
   </div>
   ```

✔ Tip

- More information on include tags can be found at the WordPress codex at http://codex.wordpress.org/Include_Tags.

Comments.php

Figure 11.12 Our theme doesn't have its own comments.php template, but WordPress provides an excellent default template that it displays as though it were part of our theme.

Conditional tags

In addition to the include tags, WordPress can use conditional tags that return Boolean TRUE or FALSE values depending on what is being displayed by WordPress at the time. For example, you can use conditional tags to display only the sidebar on your blog and to hide it on other pages by having WordPress check to see if you're on the blog page (TRUE) or on a different page (FALSE).

To use conditional tags:

1. Open your index.php file in a text editor or the Edit Themes page in your WordPress admin.

2. Add the following code to your file. This will display a simple message only if the current displayed page is the front page.

```php
<?php if(is_front_page())
{
echo "Welcome to the Front page of
→ the site";
}
?>
```

3. Save and close the index.php file.

✔ Tip

■ You can find a detailed description of the various conditional tags and their uses at http://codex.wordpress.org/Conditional_Tags.

Using the Loop

The loop is the key to a WordPress theme; it is a piece of code that pulls your content from the database into your site. It's called the loop because it runs the code in a loop until all instances of the conditional HTML and PHP are satisfied. Any HTML or PHP placed inside the loop will be rendered for each post that matches the criteria within the loop tags.

The WordPress loop starts with

```
<?php if (have_posts()) : ?>
```

```
<?php while (have_posts()) :
→ the_post(); ?>
```

and ends with

```
<?php endwhile; else: ?>
```

```
<p><?php _e('Sorry, no posts matched
→ your criteria.'); ?></p>
```

```
<?php endif; ?>
```

There is *a lot* that you can do between those two blocks of code, but primarily you will need to include the template tag `<?php the_content(); ?>` inside it. This template tag (PHP function) collects information about the current post (or page) and makes it available for display.

You could simply include `<?php the_content(); ?>` in your loop, which would work, but you can do quite a bit more in there. In fact, many of the template tags only function if they are placed *inside* the loop.

Code Listing 11.1 shows the loop from the index.php template in our example theme. This block of code tells WordPress to find available posts and display them in a particular way, complete with formatting and metadata. The section at the end tells WordPress what to display if there are no posts available.

Code Listing 11.1 The WordPress loop in action: this block of code makes the magic happen on your blog.

```
Code
<?php if ( have_posts() ) : while ( have_posts() ) : the_post(); ?>

<div class="entry">
        <h2 class="entry-title"><a href="<?php the_permalink(); ?>"><?php the_title(); ?></a></h2>
        <div class="entry-body">
                <?php the_content(); ?>
                <div class="metadata">
                        <span class="author">By <?php the_author_posts_link(); ?><span><br/>
                        <span class="date"><?php the_time('F jS, Y'); ?></span><br/>
                        <span class="categories">Categories <?php the_category(' &raquo; ');
                        ⤳ ?></span><br/>
                        <?php
                        $taglist =
get_the_tags();
                        if ($taglist) {
                                echo "<span class=\"tags\">Tags ";

        $lasttag=end($taglist);

        foreach($taglist as $val) {

        echo "<a href=\"".get_tag_link($val->term_id)."\" rel=\"tag\">".$val->name."</a>";

                if($val !== $lasttag){echo ", ";}
                                        }
                                echo "</span>";
                                }
                        ?>
                </div>
        </div>
</div>

<?php endwhile; else: ?>
<p><?php _e('Sorry, no posts matched your criteria.'); ?></p>
<?php endif; ?>
```

Validating Your Theme

Make sure your template is functioning as well as it can by validating your code. A valid theme complies with a widely accepted set of standards used by designers, Web browsers, and operating systems, which will ensure that your site is viewed correctly by your visitors.

The easiest way to check the validity of your code is to run it through a theme validator. Not all validation services check for the same things—some only look at CSS, for example, while others focus on HTML—so you may need to run more than one. We're going to walk you through the process of using the World Wide Web Consortium (W3C) validation tools so you can choose exactly what you need.

To use the W3C validation tools:

1. Navigate to the W3C Web site at www.w3.org/QA/Tools/.

2. Click the link for the first validation tool you want to use. For this example, we're starting with the MarkUp Validator (**Figure 11.13**).

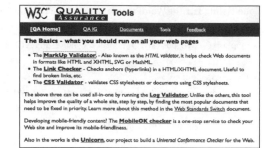

Figure 11.13 The W3C Markup Validator.

What's the W3C?

The World Wide Web Consortium (W3C) is an international group that works with the public to develop Web standards. By publishing open, nonproprietary Internet standards, the W3C helps Web technologies maintain compatibility with each other. Learn more about the W3C by visiting their Web site at www.w3.org.

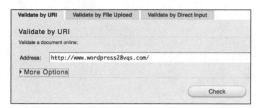

Figure 11.14 The W3C Validator is simple to use and well worth the effort. Just enter your URL and click Check to ascertain the validity of your site's code.

3. In the Address box, enter the URL of the site you want to validate (**Figure 11.14** and click Check.

You will see a report on the validity of your code. If there are errors, you will see the total number at the top of the screen (**Figure 11.15**) and a detailed list of the problems along with possible solutions below (**Figure 11.16**).

continues on next page

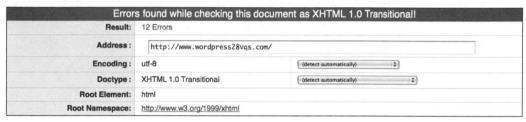

Figure 11.15 Although you can't tell from this screen shot, the Validator color-codes these results (green for pass, red for fail).

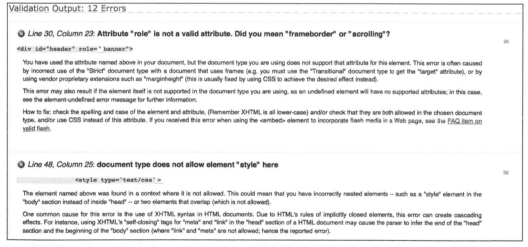

Figure 11.16 The W3C Markup Validator details any errors it finds to make them easier to correct.

4. Correct your errors and rerun the validator, if necessary.

   For example, our test run showed an error on Line 30, Column 23, in which the attribute `role` was used incorrectly. If we open the header.php file in a text editor and edit the code to remove the `role="banner"` section and save the file, that error will disappear the next time we validate the site.

5. Follow steps 2–4 to run other validators on the W3C site to make sure your site is shipshape.

12

MORE THAN A BLOG

Maintaining and updating a Web site no longer requires a degree in computer science, but typically you need to know at least a bit of HTML in order to make any significant changes to your content—or you may need to hire someone to manage the site for you. That's not always practical for an individual or a small business.

The content management system (CMS) was born in response to a growing number of site owners who did not have the time or inclination to learn code. With a CMS, it's easy to make changes to a site without modifying or even looking at the code.

In this chapter we'll show you how to use WordPress as a basic CMS to set up a static home page. We'll tell you how to set up multiple authors, and give you an overview of some popular third-party services you can use to liven up your site. We'll also provide a primer on ad integration.

WordPress as a CMS

The clean, easy-to-use administrative back end makes WordPress ideal to use as a basic CMS. WordPress sites have built-in search features and archives, and give you the ability to modify, add, and delete content without having to know a lick of code.

Since WordPress was developed originally as a blogging platform, you should make some changes to the way it displays in order to give it less of a "bloggy" feel. You'll want to set up a static home page (so that when people enter your site they will come to a page rather than directly to your blog) and tweak the URL structure to look more "friendly" by displaying categories and post names rather than a numerical string. Fortunately, WordPress already has some features in place that make this process simple.

To set up a static home page:

1. In the sidebar of your WordPress Dashboard, click Pages to expand the Pages menu and then click Add New (**Figure 12.1**).

2. On the Add New Page screen, name your new page (we called ours "Home," but you can name it whatever you want), and in the text field, enter the content you want on your home page. Click Publish at the far right (**Figure 12.2**).

Figure 12.1 Click Pages > Add New.

What's a CMS?

A content management system (CMS) is a software application that allows users to easily update and manage the content of a site without accessing or changing the site's layout and structure.

A CMS gives users an easy way to add text, images, and media, and to update and change that information on a regular basis. It typically features a search function, enabling end users to easily find the content they are looking for.

WORDPRESS AS A CMS

3. Repeating steps 1 and 2, create a new page and name it **Blog** or **Posts** (or whatever you want to call your blog section). Leave the content section blank (**Figure 12.3**). Click Publish.

continued on next page

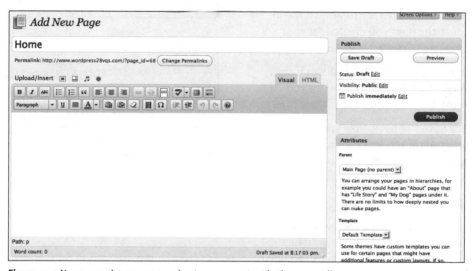

Figure 12.2 Name your home page and enter your content in the page editor.

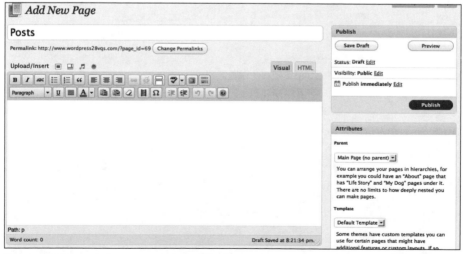

Figure 12.3 Create another new page and call it whatever you want your blog section to be called. Leave the content section blank and click Publish.

WORDPRESS AS A CMS

4. In the Dashboard sidebar, click Settings to expand the Settings menu and then click Reading (**Figure 12.4**).

5. In the Front Page Displays section of the Reading Settings page, select the "A static page (select below)" radio button (**Figure 12.5**).

6. From the Front Page drop-down menu, choose the page you created for your home page ("Home" in our example).

7. From the Posts Page drop-down menu, choose the page you created for your blog posts ("Posts" in our example).

8. Click Save Changes. Now your URL will open your new home page as the main page of your site, and your users can click Posts to access your blog.

✔ Tip

■ If you don't want to display a blog on your site at all, choose a page for your home page and leave the Posts Page drop-down option blank. Your blog posts won't be deleted, but they won't appear anywhere on your site.

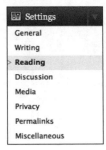

Figure 12.4 Under Settings in the sidebar, click Reading.

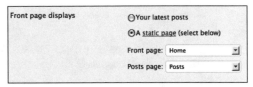

Figure 12.5 Choose your new pages from the drop-down menus to set a static front page.

Figure 12.6 Click Settings and then Permalinks to edit your permalink structure.

Figure 12.7 Enter the shortcode in the custom structure text box to change the way your links are displayed.

http://www.wordpress28vqs.com/music/music-and-memory/

Figure 12.8 Your new URL structure will use categories and post names, making your URLs more user- and search engine-friendly.

WordPress automatically generates a URL string for each new post or page. By default, these URL strings look something like this:

wordpress28vqs.com/?post_id=1

Not very memorable, is it? However, with one simple change of settings, your links can look like this:

wordpress28vqs.com/pictures/
➞ photo-gallery/

In addition to being easy to remember, this URL can help your search engine ranking, since the category and post name appear right in the post's address.

To set up friendly URLs you'll need to make a change to the way WordPress handles *permalinks* (permanent links back to your content).

To set up "friendly" URLs:

1. In the sidebar of your WordPress Dashboard, click Settings to expand the Settings menu and then click Permalinks (**Figure 12.6**).

2. On the Settings page, select the Custom Structure radio button. In the text box, enter the following shortcode (**Figure 12.7**):

   /%category%/%postname%/

3. Click Save Changes.

   Now instead of a numeric or date-based structure, your URLs will use your categories and post names (**Figure 12.8**)—in our example, music/music-and-memory.

✔ Tip

- You can learn more about permalink structure by visiting http://codex.wordpress.org/Using_Permalinks.

WORDPRESS AS A CMS

The More, the Merrier: Multiple Authors

Lining up multiple authors from your company or organization to blog is a great way to keep the content on your site fresh and interesting.

We discuss setting up additional accounts and access levels in Chapter 3, "Managing Accounts." In the following tasks, we'll tell you how to create an author page, and then how to link to it automatically from an author's name in a post's metadata.

To create an author page template:

1. Download the archives.php file from your WordPress theme. If your theme doesn't have an archives.php file, download the index.php file instead.

2. Open the archives.php file in your preferred text editor and immediately choose File > Save As. Save the file **author.php**.

3. Directly above the WordPress loop (**Figure 12.9**), insert the following code to query the database for author information:

```
<?php
if(get_query_var('author_name')) :
    $curauth = get_userdatabylogin
    → (get_query_var('author_
    → name'));
else :
    $curauth = get_userdata
    → (get_query_var('author'));
endif;
?>
```

```
<!--START THE LOOP-->
<?php if ( have_posts() ) : while ( have_posts() ) : the_post(); ?>
```

Figure 12.9 Enter the author information database query *before* the WordPress loop begins in your template file.

4. Next, enter the following code to display the author's information:

```
<h2>About: <?php echo $curauth->
→ nickname; ?></h2>
    <dl>
        <dt>Website</dt>
        <dd><a href="<?php echo
        → $curauth->user_url;
        → ?>"><?php echo $curauth->
        → user_url; ?></a></dd>
        <dt>Profile</dt>
        <dd><?php echo $curauth->
        → user_description; ?></dd>
    </dl>
```

5. Save your author.php template and upload it to your theme directory via FTP.

Your author pages are created. Next, you need to set up your theme to link authors to their pages.

✔ Tip

- See "Using the Loop," in Chapter 11, "Advanced Theme Development," for more on the WordPress loop.

The Case for WordPress MU

What if you want to run lots of different blogs on one WordPress installation? WordPress MU (Multi-User) may be the thing for you. Designed for blog networks and large organizations, WordPress MU is the powerhouse behind WordPress.com.

Using WordPress MU, you can manage several separate blogs (each with a separate owner, users, and administrators) from a single WordPress MU installation. For example, a teacher could set up a WordPress MU account and then allow students to create their own blogs on it, or a company could have separate blogs for each of its employees. Unlike a regular WordPress setup, the additional users wouldn't be subauthors for a single blog; they'd each have a blog of their own, managed under the WordPress MU administrator's umbrella.

For more information, check out http://mu.wordpress.org/.

To link authors to their pages:

1. Open your theme's index.php file in a text editor and find the line that includes the statement `<?php the_author_link(); ?>` (**Figure 12.10**).

2. Change the statement to read `<?php the_author_posts_link(); ?>` (**Figure 12.11**).

   This code modification will change the link to the author's URL (by default, this goes to the URL in the author's profile) to open a page on your site that will display the author's profile and posts.

3. Save the file and upload it to your theme.

4. Repeat this process with the single.php template.

   Now, when you click an author's name after a post, that author's page will open (**Figure 12.12**).

```
<div class="metadata">
    <span class="author">By <?php the_author_link();?><span><br/>
```

Figure 12.10 The original author link statement in the loop.

```
<div class="metadata">
    <span class="author">By <?php the_author_posts_link(); ?><span><br/>
```

Figure 12.11 Change the author link statement to show author pages when clicked.

About: jessica

Website

http://www.wordpress28vqs.com

Profile

Jessica is a designer and illustrator with a background in writing who is currently co-authoring a book on WordPress for Peachpit Press.

Posts by jessica:

photo gallery, 21 Aug 2009 in Pictures

podcast!, 21 Aug 2009 in podcast

Music and Memory, 13 Aug 2009 in music

Figure 12.12 An author page using the author.php template.

Figure 12.13 Click the Goodies link at the bottom of the Twitter screen.

Figure 12.14 Click Widgets to access Twitter's Web site widgets.

Figure 12.15 Click My Website to add a widget to your Web site.

Figure 12.16 Click Profile Widget to customize your Twitter stream display.

Figure 12.17 You can adjust settings, appearance, and dimensions before you add the widget to your site.

Integrating Third-party Services

There are lots of third-party services that play nicely with WordPress. In this section we'll pick three of our favorites—Twitter, Flickr, and Delicious—and walk you through the process of integrating them into your WordPress site.

Note that in order for these services to work, you must have an account on each of the respective services.

To add a Twitter stream to your site:

1. Log in to Twitter.com and click Goodies at the bottom of the screen (**Figure 12.13**).

2. On the Twitter Goodies page, click Widgets (**Figure 12.14**) to access Twitter's Web site widgets. These are blocks of code generated by Twitter that you can add to your own site.

3. Under "Widgets for…" click the My Website link (**Figure 12.15**).

4. Click the Profile Widget link (**Figure 12.16**). The Customize Your Profile Widget page opens.

5. Click the links at the left to adjust settings, dimensions, and color (**Figure 12.17**).

continues on next page

INTEGRATING THIRD-PARTY SERVICES

6. Click Finish & Grab Code to display the HTML for your widget (**Figure 12.18**). Copy the code to your Clipboard (press Ctrl+C on Windows, Command+C on a Mac) (**Figure 12.19**).

7. Log in to your WordPress site, click Appearance in the sidebar, and click the Widgets link.

8. From the Available Widgets list, drag a text widget into your sidebar area (**Figure 12.20**). The widget will automatically open, giving you the option to add a title and body text.

Figure 12.18 Click Finish & Grab Code.

Figure 12.19 Copy the code so you can add it to your site

INTEGRATING THIRD-PARTY SERVICES

Figure 12.20 Drag a text widget into your sidebar.

Text ▼

Title:

Twitter

```
id: 'twtr-profile-widget',
loop: true,
width: 250,
height: 300,
theme: {
  shell: {
    background: '#3082af',
    color: '#ffffff'
  },
  tweets: {
    background: '#ffffff',
    color: '#444444',
    links: '#1985b5'
  }
}
}).render().setProfile('couldbestudios').start();
</script>
```
☐ Automatically add paragraphs.

Remove | Close   **Save**

Figure 12.21 Paste the Twitter widget code into the text widget on your site.

Figure 12.22 Your Twitter updates will now appear on your site.

9. Paste the code from Twitter's widget generator into the body of the text widget (**Figure 12.21**). Give your widget a title (optional) and click Save.

Your Twitter updates will now appear in your sidebar (**Figure 12.22**).

To add your Flickr pictures to your site:

1. Go to www.flickr.com/badge.gne and choose the type of badge (Flickr's term for a grouped photo display) you want— HTML or Flash (**Figure 12.23**). Click Next: Choose Content to continue.

2. Choose which photos to include on your badge. You can pick from your own photos, a group's photos, or everyone's photos (filtered by tag) (**Figure 12.24**). Click Next: Colors to continue.

3. Using the color picker, choose colors for the background, border, links, and text of your badge (**Figure 12.25**). Use the small preview at the bottom of the screen to refine your choices. Click Next: Preview & Get Code to continue.

4. The next screen displays the necessary code to create the badge on your site. Copy the code to your Clipboard.

5. Follow steps 7–9 of the previous task to paste the code into a text widget on your WordPress site.

   Your site will now display your Flickr images.

Figure 12.23 Choose the type of badge you want. In this example, we're creating a Flash badge.

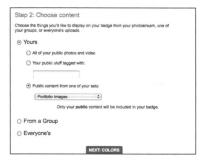

Figure 12.24 Choose which photos to include in your badge.

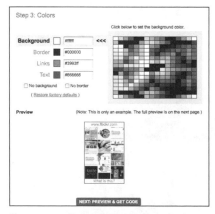

Figure 12.25 Choose colors for your badge.

Figure 12.26 Click the Settings link in your Delicious account.

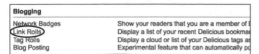

Figure 12.27 Choose Link Rolls to add a link roll (an automatically updating stream of links) to your site.

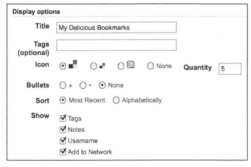

Figure 12.28 Choose the display options for your link roll, including title, icon, bullets, and sort order.

To add your Delicious links to your site:

1. Log in to your delicious.com account and click Settings (**Figure 12.26**).

2. Under Blogging, choose Link Rolls (**Figure 12.27**).

3. Choose your display options, including title, tags, icon, bullets, sort order, and what information to show.

   You will see a live preview of your link roll at the right side of the screen (**Figure 12.28**), and the code in the code box at the top of your screen will automatically update to reflect each display change.

4. Copy the code in the code box (**Figure 12.29**) to your Clipboard.

5. Follow steps 7–9 from the task "To add a Twitter stream to your site" to paste the code into a text widget on your WordPress site. Your Delicious links will now show up in your sidebar.

Linkrolls are a way for you to have your latest Delicious bookmarks displayed as part of your website. First play with the settings below then simply insert this HTML code into the hypertext of your page:

```
<script type="text/javascript" src="http://feeds.delicious.com/v2/js/couldbe?title=My%20Delicious%20Bookmarks&icon=m&count=5&sort=date&tags&extended&name&showadd"></script>
```

Figure 12.29 Copy the Delicious code and enter it into a text box on your site.

Monetize Your Site: Ad Integration

Want to make a little pocket change from your WordPress blog? One of the best ways to generate income from your Web site is through ad integration. To take advantage of one of the most popular online ad services, the Google AdSense program, you need to create an account if you don't already have one.

To add advertising to your site:

1. Sign in to your AdSense account at www.google.com/adsense (**Figure 12.30**).

2. In AdSense, click the AdSense Setup tab (**Figure 12.31**).

3. Click AdSense For Content (**Figure 12.32**).

4. Using the AdSense wizards, create the ad campaign that you wish to run on your site (**Figure 12.33**).

5. When you complete the wizard, copy the provided code (**Figure 12.34**).

   Now that you've created your ad campaign and Google has provided the necessary code, you need to set up your WordPress site to display the advertising.

6. In your WordPress admin area, click Plugins, and then click Add New. In the search box, type **Quick Adsense** and click Search Plugins.

Figure 12.30 Sign in to your AdSense account.

Figure 12.31 Click AdSense Setup to begin setup of your ad campaign.

Figure 12.32 Click the AdSense For Content link.

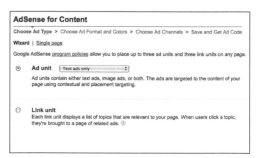

Figure 12.33 Let the AdSense wizard guide you through the process of creating your ad campaign.

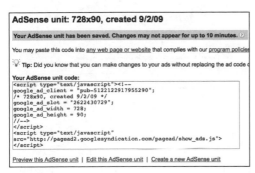

Figure 12.34 Copy the code to your Clipboard.

Figure 12.35 In your sidebar, click Settings, and then select Quick Adsense.

7. In the list of plug-ins, find Quick AdSense.

8. Click Install next to the Quick AdSense plug-in's description, and then click Install Now in the pop-up window.

9. After the plug-in downloads, click the Activate Plugin link. (For more detailed instructions on adding plug-ins, please refer to the "To add plug-ins to your blog" section in Chapter 9, "Widgets and Plug-ins.")

10. In your WordPress admin area, go to Settings > Quick Adsense (**Figure 12.35**).

11. On the Quick Adsense Settings page, enter the options for your AdSense display (**Figure 12.36**). You can choose the number of ads to place on each page, their position, and which posts and/or pages to display them on.

12. Scroll down to the Adsense Codes section (**Figure 12.37**). Paste the code you copied from Google AdSense into the first box, Ads1.

continues on next page

Figure 12.36 Choose the options for your ad display.

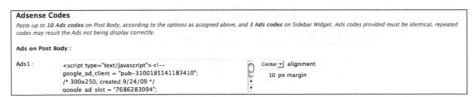

Figure 12.37 Paste your Google AdSense code into the box for Ad1. You can paste up to ten codes in the provided boxes.

MONETIZE YOUR SITE: AD INTEGRATION

13. If you want to use AdSense in a sidebar widget, enter additional code from Google AdSense here (**Figure 12.38**).

14. To complete widget setup, you will need to navigate to the Widget admin page after you've saved your settings and drag a Quick AdSense widget into your sidebar. See "Using Widgets" in Chapter 9 for more detailed instructions on widget use.

15. Click Save Changes.

Your ads will now appear on your site (**Figure 12.39**).

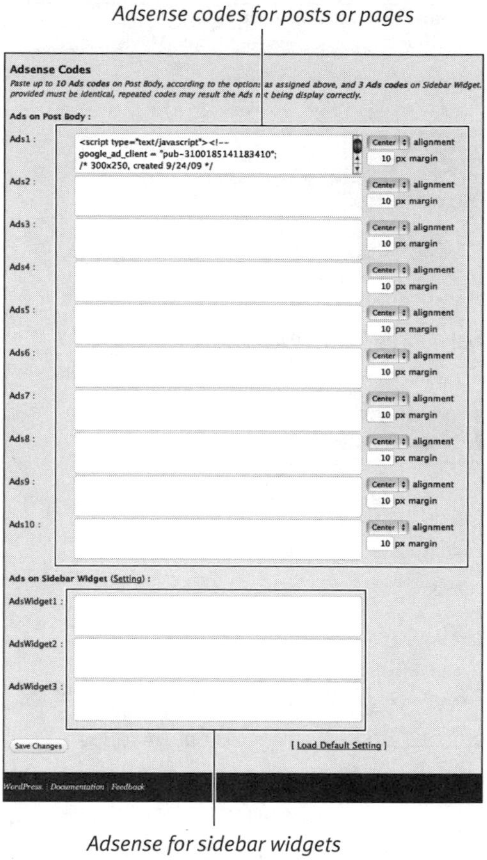

Adsense codes for posts or pages

Adsense for sidebar widgets

Figure 12.38 You can also enter AdSense code into the Ads on Sidebar Widget section to display ads in your sidebar.

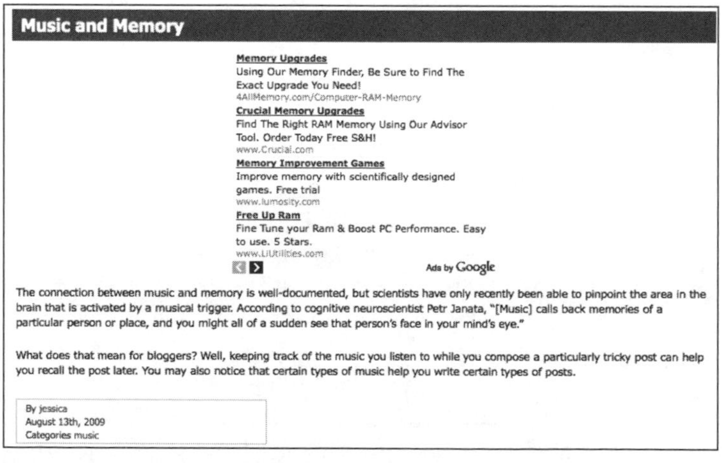

Figure 12.39 Your ad campaign will now appear on your site.

13

TOOLS AND TRICKS

Updating your site shouldn't be a chore, and there is a plethora of online tools designed to make it as simple as possible to integrate blogging into your everyday life. You can post right from your desktop (whether or not you're connected to the Internet), preview changes to your theme files, and check stats to see who's visiting your site in real time.

In this chapter, we'll walk you through the process of setting up and using some of these tools to make your blogging experience richer and more rewarding. In almost no time, you'll be blogging just like a pro!

Tools for Blogging: Different Ways to Post

The Dashboard post editor (see Chapter 4, "Adding Content") is great, but what about those times when you want to compose something on your desktop? Desktop post editors offer a way to keep your posts organized, and give you the ability to compose posts even when you're not online.

There are lots of blog post editors out there, and nearly all of them support WordPress.

✔ Tip

■ In order to use any desktop blogging tools, you must make sure the XML-RPC interface is enabled on WordPress (it's disabled by default). In the WordPress admin area, select Settings > Writing and click the XML-RPC check box in the Remote Publishing section.

Popular Post Editors

◆ **MarsEdit (Mac):** Supports WYSIWYG editing, spell check, image and file uploads, and macros. MarsEdit also integrates directly with Flickr, as well as with some popular text editors such as TextMate and SubEthaEdit. www.red-sweater.com/marsedit/

◆ **Blogo (Mac):** Lets you crop images from the editor and includes micro-blogging support for services like Twitter and Ping.fm. Blogo also supports drag-and-drop posting via a browser bookmarklet. www.drinkbrainjuice.com/blogo

◆ **Windows Live Writer (Windows):** Includes advanced image-editing features such as inserting multiple photos, tiling, and adding borders, and has optional plug-ins for Digg, Flickr, and Twitter. http://windowslivewriter.spaces.live.com/

◆ **ScribeFire (cross-platform, Firefox Extension):** Integrates with the Firefox Web browser to allow you to post to your blog directly from your browser. www.scribefire.com/

Figure 13.1 Enter your site name and URL to set up a new blog.

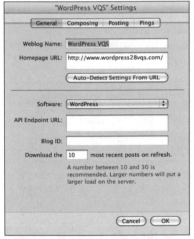

Figure 13.2 Enter your blog settings manually if they are not autodetected. You only need to worry about the name, URL, and software, so you can leave the rest blank.

Figure 13.3 The blog editor will store your username and password so you do not have to enter them each time you post.

To set up a desktop weblog editor:

1. Download or install the blog editor of your choice; for our example, we'll be using MarsEdit. Open the blog editor (see the documentation for your chosen application for specific instructions).

2. Click File > New Weblog.

3. Enter the name of your site and the URL (**Figure 13.1**).

4. If the blog editor is able to detect your settings, just click Finish and continue to step 5. Otherwise, a window will open in which you can enter your settings (**Figure 13.2**).

5. Enter your username and password to activate posting (**Figure 13.3**). Click OK.

TOOLS FOR BLOGGING: DIFFERENT WAYS TO POST

To post by e-mail:

1. Open your e-mail client of choice (in this example, we'll be using Gmail) (**Figure 13.4**).

2. Create a new e-mail using your secret "post-by-mail" e-mail address (if you haven't set this up already, please follow the instructions in Appendix A) (**Figure 13.5**).

3. Enter a subject line for your e-mail. This will become the title of your post.

4. Enter your post content in the body of your e-mail in plain text (**Figure 13.6**).

5. Click Send. The new post will appear on your site (**Figure 13.7**).

Figure 13.4 Open the e-mail client of your choice to create a new message.

Figure 13.5 Your secret e-mail address will post directly to your blog, so don't share it with anyone!

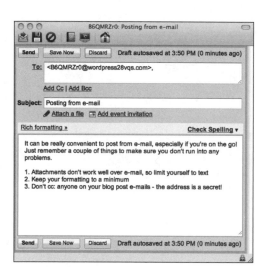

Figure 13.6 Use plain text for your blog post e-mails, and avoid attachments to make sure you don't run into any problems such as garbled code, incorrect formatting, or missing graphics.

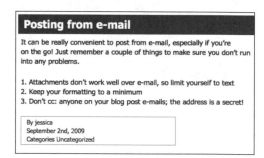

Figure 13.7 Your e-mail will show up on your site as a new post.

SEO: What You Need to Know

One modification people are often eager to make to themes is the addition of SEO (Search Engine Optimization) features. Here are some tips for optimizing your WordPress site:

◆ Don't block search engine traffic. Make sure you're letting search engines find you by selecting Settings > Privacy and choosing the option "I would like my blog to be visible to everyone, including search engines (like Google, Sphere, Technorati) and archivers" (**Figure 13.8**).

◆ Make sure your code is valid. Mistakes in your HTML could have negative consequences in search engine ranking. Run your code through a validator (more on that in Chapter 11, "Advanced Theme Development") and repair any errors that come up.

◆ Install a site map plug-in like Google XML Sitemap Generator (http://wordpress.org/extend/plugins/google-sitemap-generator/) to create a search engine-friendly site map.

◆ Use keywords in your posts and pages, but don't go crazy—blatant overuse of keywords and phrases can actually drive traffic away from your site.

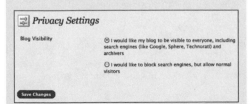

Figure 13.8 Make sure you aren't blocking search engine traffic! Select Settings > Privacy and choose the appropriate option.

Tools for Modifying Theme Files

There are two ways to make significant changes to a theme:

◆ You can use the built-in theme editor as discussed in Chapter 8, "Customizing Your WordPress Theme."

or

◆ You can download the theme you wish to modify using your favorite FTP client, edit the files directly using the plain-text code editor of your choice, and re-upload them to activate your changes.

If you're using a plain-text editor, it's best to pair it with a browser extension such as Firefox's Firebug (http://getfirebug.com), which allows you to view styles and preview changes right in your browser.

In this section, we'll show you how to use a browser extension in conjunction with a plain-text code editor to preview and make changes to a theme's style sheet.

✔ Tips

■ Theme files are stored in wp-content/themes in your WordPress installation directory.

■ We highly recommend TextMate (http://macromates.com) for editing code on the Mac, and Notepad++ (http://notepad-plus.sourceforge.net) for Windows computers.

To use a browser extension to preview code changes:

Figure 13.9 Click the bug icon to activate Firebug.

1. Open your site in Firefox and click the bug icon in the lower right of your browser window to activate Firebug (**Figure 13.9**). A split pane will open in your browser, with Firebug beneath your open site (**Figure 13.10**).

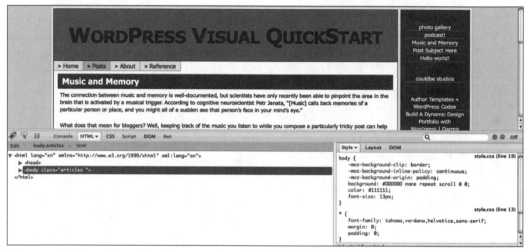

Figure 13.10 Firebug will open in a split pane in your browser.

Figure 13.11
Click the box with the arrow to activate the Element Inspector.

2. Click the Element Inspector (**Figure 13.11**) and move your mouse over elements of your site.

   You will see a box surrounding each of your site elements as you mouse over them. Each element will show the corresponding HTML on the left side of the Firebug pane, while the CSS will appear on the right side (**Figure 13.12**).

3. Click once on the element you would like to view. This stops the boxes from appearing around your content and freezes the code in place.

continues on next page

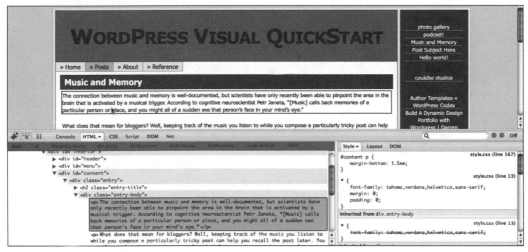

Figure 13.12 When you mouse over a section of your site, you will see a box appear around each element while the CSS and HTML for that element appears in the Firebug pane.

4. To preview a CSS modification, click the CSS property you want to modify on the right side of the Firebug pane. It will become editable (**Figure 13.13**); if you enter a modification (such as *margin-bottom: 1.5em*) in the editable area of the Firebug pane, it will preview on your site in the main screen (**Figure 13.14**).

   In this example, we added 20 pixels of padding to either side of each paragraph in the content area. (Don't worry; this won't affect your actual site—it's for previewing purposes only.)

5. Once you know what elements you'd like to change, go ahead and open your style sheet in your text editor.

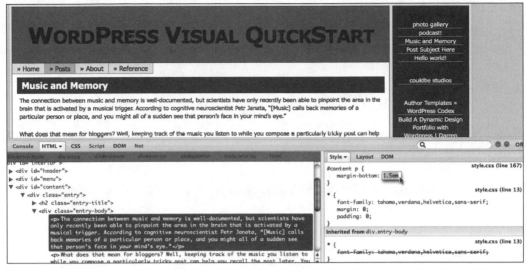

Figure 13.13 Clicking a property in Firebug will make it editable, allowing you to make changes and see them right away.

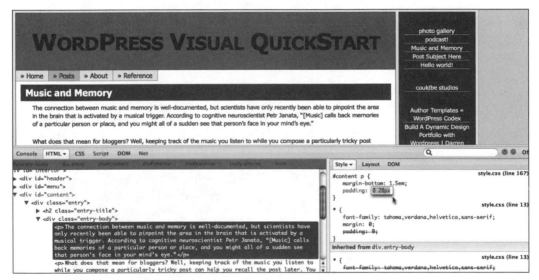

Figure 13.14 Changes you make in Firebug will preview on your site. In this example, we added 20 pixels of padding to each side of the content's paragraphs, making them indent on either side.

To edit a style sheet via FTP:

1. Download your theme's style sheet (often called style.css) to your computer and open it in your preferred text editor.

2. Locate the style declaration (such as *#content p*) you'd like to modify.

   If you've been using a browser extension like Firebug to preview changes, you can see the line number of the style declaration right in the Firebug pane (**Figure 13.15**). If not, you can always search for the CSS property's name.

3. Make your changes and save your file.

4. Re-upload the file via FTP to your theme directory.

```
#content p {                              style.css (line 167)
    margin-bottom: 1.5em;
    padding: 0 20px;
}
```

Figure 13.15 You can see the line number of the style you modified in Firebug so you can easily locate it on your actual style sheet.

Directly Accessing the Database

Sometimes you may find that you want to adjust something directly in your database. Doing so with WordPress is fairly straightforward if you know MySQL.

A well-maintained schema with references and diagrams for the WordPress database structure can be found at http://codex. wordpress.org/Database_Description.

Generally speaking, directly hacking the database should be a tool of last resort for you, especially since your changes will be lost when you upgrade to a newer version of WordPress! But the option is always there and can be especially useful when troubleshooting the rare or esoteric problems that can come up.

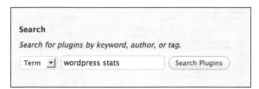

Figure 13.16 Click Add New in the Plugins menu to start the process of finding a new plug-in.

Figure 13.17 Find the WordPress.com Stats plug-in by searching for it.

Figure 13.18 Locate the WordPress.com Stats plug-in in the list of available plug-ins and click Install.

Using Stats to Evaluate Traffic

You can get valuable information about your site by checking out statistics showing who is visiting your site, how they got there, and which pages they're viewing.

Lots of stats-viewing add-ons are available. We'll show you how to install Stats, the one developed by Automattic, the company behind WordPress. This plug-in accesses your WordPress database to give you up-to-date stats, and it's hosted on the WordPress.com servers so it will not slow down your site's performance.

To install the Stats plug-in:

1. In the sidebar menu of your admin screen, select Plugins and click Add New (**Figure 13.16**).

2. In the search box on the New Plugins page, enter **wordpress stats** (**Figure 13.17**).

3. Find the WordPress.com Stats plug-in in the list (**Figure 13.18**) and click the Install link at the far right.

continues on next page

USING STATS TO EVALUATE TRAFFIC

4. Click the Install Now link on the pop-up window (**Figure 13.19**). A message will appear telling you that the plug-in has been successfully installed (**Figure 13.20**).

5. Click the Activate Plugin link below the success message.

This will bring you to your Manage Plugins screen, where you will see a message saying that your plug-in has been activated as well as a message saying *WordPress.com Stats needs attention: please enter an API key or disable the plugin.*

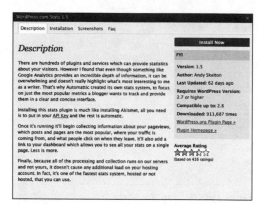

Figure 13.19 Click the Install Now button in the pop-up window to install the plug-in.

Figure 13.20 Success! Your plug-in has been installed.

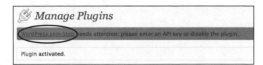

Figure 13.21 Click the link to open the WordPress Stats configuration screen.

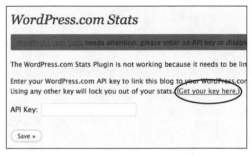

Figure 13.22 Enter your WordPress.com API key to activate the WordPress.com Stats plug-in.

Figure 13.23 Blog Stats are now activated on your site. You can access them at any time by clicking the Blog Stats link in the sidebar of your admin area.

6. Click the WordPress.com Stats link (**Figure 13.21**) in the message to open the WordPress.com Stats configuration screen.

7. Enter your WordPress.com API key.

If you don't have one, click the Get Your Key Here link (**Figure 13.22**) to visit the WordPress.com site and sign up for a free account. (For more information about getting an API key from WordPress.com, please see the "Fighting Spam with Akismet" section in Chapter 5.)

8. A Blog Stats link will appear in the sidebar menu below the link to your Dashboard (**Figure 13.23**). Click the link to see statistics whenever you log in to the administrative section of your site. You can view stats on your views per day, top referrers, most viewed posts and pages, and more.

CUSTOMIZE YOUR SETTINGS

One of the greatest things about WordPress is the way it can be customized. Without entering a smidgeon of code, you can choose how many posts are displayed, pick a static page for your front page, add or change your site's title and tagline, and set sizes for your uploaded images and thumbnails.

You can access all of the settings for your WordPress blog site through the sidebar menu, under Settings (**Figure A.1**).

Figure A.1 You'll find the Settings command all the way at the bottom of the sidebar. Click Settings to expand the submenu.

Working with the General Settings

The General Settings page contains a variety of basic information about your site and how it is configured (**Figure A.2**). This is the place to choose default new user settings, set your time zone, and choose the way you want times and dates displayed.

◆ **Blog Title:** This is the title of your site. You originally set this title when you installed WordPress, but you can change it here. Almost all themes will display this title somewhere on your site, most often as the main title in the header at the top of your site, as well as in the `<title>` tag that displays at the top of your browser window in the title bar. WordPress will also use this as the title of your syndication (RSS) feeds.

◆ **Tagline:** The tagline of your blog is usually just a sentence that briefly describes your blog. By default, Tagline will be set to "Just another WordPress weblog." Themes typically use this as part of the meta-description for your site and/or as part of your header as a subheading beneath your blog title. This functions like a corporate slogan that appears beside a logo.

◆ **WordPress address (URL):** This setting is the URL that points to your WordPress installation location. Typically, this will be the same as the blog address. It can be used in conjunction with the blog address if you want to run WordPress from an alternate location inside your site.

◆ **Blog address (URL):** The blog address is used if you want to install WordPress into one directory but run the site from a different directory. For example, you might install WordPress at yoursite.com/wordpress but want the site to be

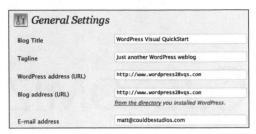

Figure A.2 The top half of the General Settings screen, where you can customize your blog title, tagline, URL, and e-mail address.

displayed at just yoursite.com. To do this, enter into the Blog address field the URL that you want your users to enter in their browser. Click the "...to be different from the directory..." link below the blog address to view the detailed instructions for setting this up at http://codex.wordpress.org/Giving_WordPress_Its_Own_Directory.

◆ **E-mail address:** Enter the e-mail address that you want WordPress to use when it e-mails you for administrative tasks such as comment moderation and new user notification.

◆ **Membership:** If you select the Membership option (**Figure A.3**), visitors to your site will be able to create their own accounts. Usually this is just a subscriber account that allows them to comment on your blog posts; the default account level is defined in the next step.

continues on next page

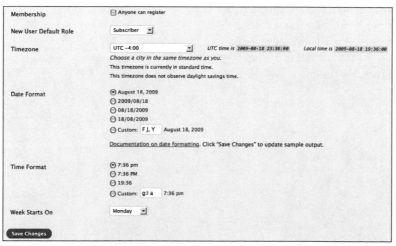

Figure A.3 The lower half of the General Settings screen, where you can customize membership and subscriber options and time and date format.

WORKING WITH THE GENERAL SETTINGS

◆ **New User Default Role:** By default, this will be set to Subscriber, but you can choose to default new users to the role of Author, Editor, or even Administrator. Be careful in changing this, especially if you have the Membership check box set to allow anyone to register.

◆ **Timezone:** You can adjust the Timezone information to ensure that the dates and time used on your blog posts and within WordPress match your local time.

◆ **Date Format:** This allows you to adjust how WordPress displays dates. Select one of the default settings or choose custom formatting rules. Note that WordPress uses the same settings for custom date strings as are used in the `date()` function in PHP.

◆ **Time Format:** You can customize the way WordPress processes times by adjusting the Time Format setting.

◆ **Week Starts On:** WordPress can display calendars marking your updates. Use the Week Starts On option to set the point at which the week starts for those calendars. By default, it will be set to Monday, so if you want your calendars to display Sunday through Saturday, set Week Starts On to Sunday.

Customizing Content Creation

The Writing Settings page (**Figure A.4**) is used to configure how you create content such as blog posts on your site. You can specify everything from the size of the post box to your remote posting settings here.

Writing Settings

Size of the post box	10 lines
Formatting	☑ Convert emoticons like :-) and :-P to graphics on display ☐ WordPress should correct invalidly nested XHTML automatically
Default Post Category	Uncategorized ▾
Default Link Category	Blogroll ▾

Remote Publishing

To post to WordPress from a desktop blogging client or remote website that uses the Atom Publishing Protocol or one of the XML-RPC publishing interfaces you must enable them below.

Atom Publishing Protocol	☐ Enable the Atom Publishing Protocol.
XML-RPC	☐ Enable the WordPress, Movable Type, MetaWeblog and Blogger XML-RPC publishing protocols.

Post via e-mail

To post to WordPress by e-mail you must set up a secret e-mail account with POP3 access. Any mail received at this address will be posted, so it's a good idea to keep this address very secret. Here are three random strings you could use: R0V7Dltu , 9t0ZISGs , oPTtvLE2 .

Mail Server	mail.example.com Port 110
Login Name	login@example.com
Password	password
Default Mail Category	Uncategorized ▾

Update Services

When you publish a new post, WordPress automatically notifies the following site update services. For more about this, see Update Services on the Codex. Separate multiple service URLs with line breaks.

http://rpc.pingomatic.com/

Figure A.4 Customize your writing settings here.

◆ **Size of the post box:** This controls the size of the box that you use to type your blog posts and pages. By default, it is set to 10 lines, which should work for most people; however, you can change the setting if you prefer more or less space. If you primarily post to your blog from a small laptop, for example, you might want to use a smaller post box, whereas if you use a large desktop monitor you may want it larger.

◆ **Formatting:** You can enable "smileys" and other emoticons for your site (**Figure A.5**, **Figure A.6**), or instruct WordPress to correct invalid XHTML markup in your posts.

◆ **Default Post Category:** When you create a new post, it is assigned to a category. If you didn't select a category when you created the post, it will be assigned to the default category, which in a new WordPress installation is Uncategorized. You can set it to any of your categories (for more information on categories, check out Chapter 4, "Adding Content").

◆ **Default Link Category:** When you add links to your site, they are automatically assigned to the default category, Blogroll. You may want to change this to reflect what you actually link to (for example, you could call it Links).

◆ **Remote Publishing:** Various blogging software applications are available that you can use to post content to your site; if you want to use one of them, you can enable the protocol required by your client application here (**Figure A.7**).

Figure A.5 Emoticons in text form.

Figure A.6 WordPress can convert text emoticons into graphics in your posts.

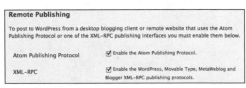

Figure A.7 Remote Publishing settings on the Writing Settings page.

Figure A.8 Set up your "post via e-mail" settings here, using a secret e-mail address. WordPress provides some random account names as ideas.

◆ **Post via e-mail:** WordPress has the ability to accept blog posts via e-mail. In order for it to work, you will need to set up an e-mail account for your site. You must know the server settings for your POP3 e-mail account to set this up. Because items sent to this address will be posted on your site, the e-mail address you choose should never be shared or used for purposes other than posting. The account name should also be difficult to guess. To help you with this, WordPress lists a few randomized strings that you could use for account names (**Figure A.8**).

◆ **Update Services:** WordPress supports XML-RPC ping services that let other Web sites know when you update your blog. These services can be helpful in driving traffic to your site. You can find a list of other ping services at http://codex. wordpress.org/Update_Services.

Customizing WordPress Display

The Reading Settings page (**Figure A.9**) allows you to control aspects of how WordPress displays your content. Choose whether your blog or a static page is the first thing new visitors see, set the number of posts per page, and customize your feed settings here.

◆ **Front page displays:** By default, your blog will display your recent blog posts on the front page of the site; however, if you are using WordPress primarily as a content management system, you can select alternate pages for WordPress to display for your home page and blog posts (**Figure A.10**).

◆ **Blog pages show at most:** This indicates the maximum number of posts shown on one page when reading the blog.

◆ **Syndication feeds show the most recent:** This specifies the number of posts included in your RSS or other syndication feeds. It defaults to 10 posts.

◆ **For each article in a feed, show:** You can control whether your WordPress site sends out your feed with full blog posts or just a summary of the posts, requiring a click-through to read the entire content.

◆ **Encoding for pages and feeds:** If you need to use a character encoding for your site other than UTF-8, you can specify that here.

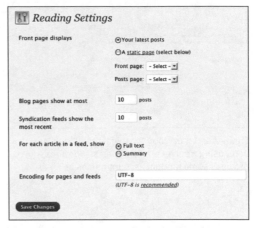

Figure A.9 Customize your display settings here. You can choose how your blog looks to visitors and how your feed appears to people viewing it on a feed reader.

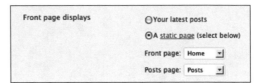

Figure A.10 You can choose a static front page here, so visitors to your site will see a page rather than going directly to your blog.

Setting Comment Controls

The Discussion Settings page is used primarily to control how WordPress handles comments on your blog, although it also allows you to configure pingbacks, trackbacks, and user avatars (user icons).

◆ **Default article settings:** These are used to control incoming and outgoing pingbacks and trackbacks, and to control whether commenting is enabled by default (**Figure A.11**).

◆ **Other comment settings:** These control what steps a user needs to take before he or she is allowed to comment on your blog posts, and how comments are displayed when there are a large number of them (**Figure A.12**).

◆ **E-mail me whenever:** Use this setting to control how often you receive e-mail from WordPress when your blog gets new comments.

continues on next page

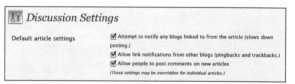

Figure A.11 Toggle the check boxes to select and deselect options for pingbacks, trackbacks, and whether commenting is enabled by default.

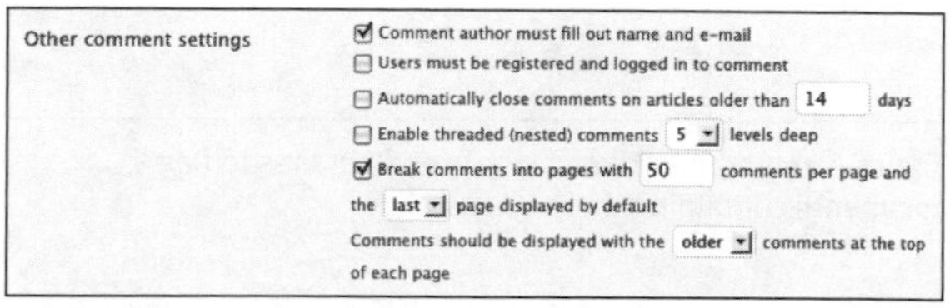

Figure A.12 You can set the rules for commenting here, including what it takes for a reader to be allowed to comment and how many comments are displayed at once.

◆ **Before a comment appears:** These are comment approval settings. By default, user comments are held for moderation unless the user has had a comment approved previously (**Figure A.13**).

◆ **Comment Moderation:** You can control what comments are held in the moderation queue (covered in Chapter 5, "Moderating Comments") by adding words to watch out for and limiting the number of links allowed in a comment.

◆ **Comment Blacklist:** You can ban certain words from comments. Anything you enter in this box will cause comments that contain the word to be automatically flagged as spam (**Figure A.14**).

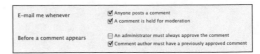

Figure A.13 Want to moderate your comments before they go live? Choose approval settings here.

Figure A.14 Add blacklisted words and phrases to flag comments containing them as spam.

◆ **Avatars:** You can control whether you allow avatars (user icons) on your site. You can also set restrictions on the content of the icons as well as a default picture to use for users who don't have an avatar set up (**Figure A.15**). WordPress uses the Gravatar service (www.gravatar. com); users who have set up an account with Gravatar will see their user icon on your site if you enable this feature.

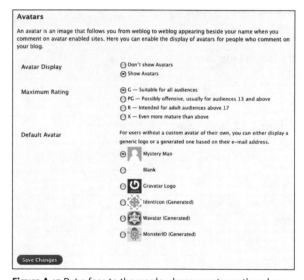

Figure A.15 Put a face to the words: choose avatar options here.

Additional Settings

The settings that follow aren't vital to your site's functionality, but they can make a big difference in the way your site handles things like images, search engines, permalinks, and uploads.

Media Settings

The Media Settings page (**Figure A.16**) controls the size of the image thumbnails and scaled-down versions of images you upload to your posts. The standard setting for this is a 150-by-150-pixel thumbnail, a 300-square-pixel medium-size image, and a large size of up to 1024 by 1024 pixels.

Privacy Settings

The Privacy Settings (**Figure A.17**) allow you to hide your site from search engines if you so desire.

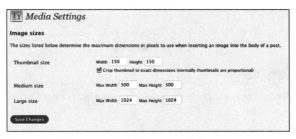

Figure A.16 Set your default image sizes here.

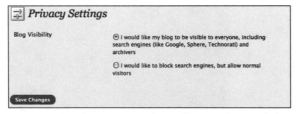

Figure A.17 If you want to block search engine traffic, you can do so in the Privacy Settings.

Permalink Settings

The Permalink Settings (**Figure A.18**) are used to control the way that WordPress builds URLs to your pages and blog posts.

The default setting uses yoursite.com/?p=*123*, where *123* is a numeric identifier for your content. However, there are good reasons to change this to an alternate permalink structure. The alternatives are both more informative to humans looking at the URL, as well as to search engines that crawl your site.

◆ **Common settings:** You can select one of the standard permalink structures, or you can create a custom permalink structure. Click the "A number of tags are available" link to find out more about creating custom permalink structures.

◆ **Optional:** You can also customize the permalinks used for categories and tags.

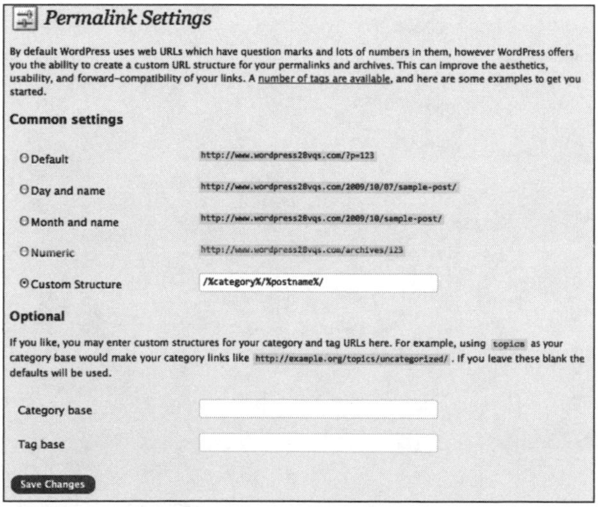

Figure A.18 Change permalinks to a predefined default or make your own custom structure.

Miscellaneous Settings

The Miscellaneous Settings page controls the location and folder structure WordPress uses to store uploaded files and whether or not to keep track of the update times of links (**Figure A.19**).

Figure A.19 Settings that aren't covered in other sections, such as folder structure for uploaded files and link update tracking settings, can be customized here.

TROUBLESHOOTING B

In this section, we'll help out with some common WordPress problems and point you in the right direction for finding answers online.

My changes aren't showing up

Have you emptied your cache? Sometimes, to save time and resources, your browser will show you a previously captured, or *cached*, version of a page. You can clear your browser cache and force the page to reload by following these instructions:

Microsoft Internet Explorer

◆ Hold down Shift and click the Refresh button in the toolbar.

For serious clearing: If you are having problems clearing out the cache, you can force it by choosing Tools > Delete Browsing History to open the Delete Browsing History dialog box (**Figure B.1**). Select the Temporary Internet Files check box and click Delete.

Mozilla Firefox

◆ Hold down Ctrl+Shift+R (Command+Shift+R on a Mac).

For serious clearing: From the browser's menu, choose Tools and select Clear Recent History. In the drop-down menu for "Time range to clear," select Everything and click "Clear Now."

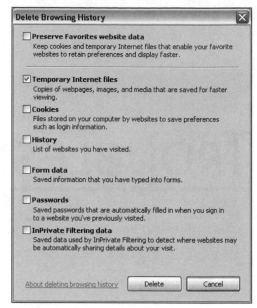

Figure B.1 To empty your cache in Internet Explorer 8, click Tools > Delete Browsing History, select Temporary Internet Files, and click Delete.

Figure B.2 Reset Safari by clicking Safari > Reset Safari.

Opera

◆ From the browser's menu, choose Edit > File > Preferences. Choose History and Cache and click Cache.

Safari

◆ From the browser's menu, choose Safari > Reset Safari (**Figure B.2**) and click Reset to confirm.

or

Choose Safari > Empty Cache.

(Note that this browser is generally used with a Mac, though these instructions also work for the Windows version.)

All Browsers

If the previous troubleshooting tips don't solve the problem, check your source code. Something as simple as a tag that was never closed can keep a page from loading correctly. If you don't find any problems, run your page through a validator to see if any errors come up. (For more information on validation, see Chapter 11, "Advanced Theme Development.")

If none of these methods works for you, check out the detailed instructions on the WordPress Codex for more in-depth troubleshooting: http://codex.wordpress.org/I_Make_Changes_and_Nothing_Happens.

TROUBLESHOOTING

Changes I made to the WordPress default theme were lost during the last automatic upgrade!

A core upgrade copies all the new files from the distribution over the old ones—including files in the WordPress default theme. That means if you changed existing files in the WordPress default theme (e.g., the CSS file found at wp-content/themes/default/style.css), those changes got overwritten when you upgraded. There isn't a fix for this, but we can offer advice to make sure it doesn't happen again!

To prevent loss of theme changes during an upgrade:

1. If you are customizing the default theme, make a copy of the entire theme directory, rename it, and upload it as a new theme. This will prevent it from being overwritten during an upgrade, since the only theme affected by upgrades is the WordPress default theme.

2. After you copy the theme directory, change the comment block at the top of the style.css file to differentiate it from the default theme. In other words, replace Theme Name: WordPress Default with something like Theme Name: WordPress Default Modified.

✔ Tip

■ Always back up your files and database before an update.

An update to WordPress was just released, so why doesn't my blog recognize that the update is available?

Looking for that release notification at the top of your administrative panel? Not every blog will see that message at the same time. Your blog is programmed to check for updates every 12 hours, so if an update was released right after the last check, it may be a while before you are notified.

You can force the issue if you really need that update right away.

To update your blog before you receive an update notification:

1. In your Web-hosting control panel, access the MySQL database for your WordPress installation.

2. In the MySQL database, delete the `update_core` option name record in your *wp_options* table. That will cause your WordPress installation to check immediately for an update rather than waiting the remainder of the time from the last check.

I can't access the administrative menus!

If you were able to access the admin menu in the past but can't now, a bad plug-in may be to blame. To identify the culprit, you'll need to deactivate all your plug-ins, and then add them back one by one. But how do you deactivate your plug-ins if you can't get to the admin menu? You have two options.

To deactivate all plug-ins:

1. Use phpMyAdmin or another database administration tool to access your database directly.

2. In the MySQL table *wp_options*, under the *option_name* column (field), find the *active_plugins* row.

3. Change the *option_value* field value to **a:0:{}**.
   This forces all your plug-ins to register as inactive.

or

1. Create an empty plugins folder on your computer.

2. Via FTP or your host's control panel, navigate to the wp-content folder (directory).

3. Via FTP or your host's control panel, rename the plugins folder to plugins.hold (**Figure B.3**).

4. Via FTP or your host's control panel, create a new folder called plugins in the wp-content directory (**Figure B.4**).

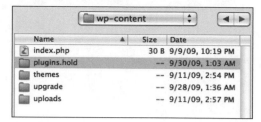

Figure B.3 Navigate to your wp-content folder and rename your plugins folder to plugins.hold.

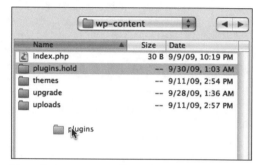

Figure B.4 Create a new (empty) folder called plugins in your wp-content directory.

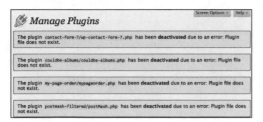

Figure B.5 The empty plugins folder causes WordPress to show all your plug-ins as deactivated.

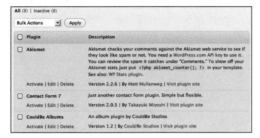

Figure B.6 Once you restore your original plugins folder, WordPress will give you the option to reactivate all your plug-ins.

5. Log in to your WordPress admin menu and click Plugins. Since your plugins folder is empty, WordPress automatically deactivates all your plug-ins (**Figure B.5**).

6. Via FTP or your host's control panel, delete the empty plugins folder you previously created.

7. Via FTP or your host's control panel, rename plugins.hold back to plugins.

8. In your administration screen, refresh the Plugins section. You will see all your old plug-ins in the list ready for you to activate them (**Figure B.6**).

9. Activate plug-ins one by one to find the culprit that caused the initial access problem.

Why do I get a blank page when I submit a comment?

If a blank page appears when a comment is submitted and the comment does not show up on your site, your theme may be missing a critical part of the comment form. Check the comments.php file in your theme and ensure that the following code appears within the form:

```
<input type="hidden" name="comment_
→ post_ID" value="<?php echo $id; ?>" />
```

If the code is not there, enter it just below the code for the Submit button.

Where do I go for help?

If you get stuck with a WordPress problem you can't easily resolve, there are lots of ways to find the answers you need:

◆ Get online and start researching. The WordPress site provides user forums and excellent documentation that can offer the assistance you need.

◆ If you have a specific error or problem, try inputting the error message directly into a search engine, especially the blog search function of Google. Bloggers love to talk about the technology behind their blogs, and many people will post explanations of problems they have resolved on their own sites.

◆ Get to know the other WordPress users in your local area; they can be a great resource. Many regional groups maintain their own forums or mailing lists where you can get help from people who might be willing to go a little bit further for another local than might be expected in larger communities.

TROUBLESHOOTING

Online Help Resources

◆ WordPress Codex: Troubleshooting FAQ: http://codex.wordpress.org/FAQ_Troubleshooting

◆ WordPress Forums: http://wordpress.org/support/

◆ Local user group listings http://wordpress.meetup.com/

Or search for "WordPress User Group, {*your town*}" to check for other local sites.

◆ Google blog search: http://blogsearch.google.com

ONLINE RESOURCES

Here is a list of Web sites that can provide valuable information about WordPress, blogging, and our recommended software.

For a comprehensive list of resources, you can visit this book's companion site at http://wordpress28vqs.com.

WordPress Information

WordPress (official site):
http://wordpress.org

WordPress.com:
http://wordpress.com

WordPress Codex:
http://codex.wordpress.org

WordPress Forums:
http://wordpress.org/support

WordPress Requirements:
http://wordpress.org/about/requirements

WordPress Web Hosting:
http://wordpress.org/hosting

Using Themes:
http://codex.wordpress.org/Using_Themes

Free Themes Directory:
http://wordpress.org/extend/themes

Templates:
http://codex.wordpress.org/Templates

Template Hierarchy:
http://codex.wordpress.org/Template_Hierarchy

Template Tags:
http://codex.wordpress.org/Template_Tags

Using Permalinks:
http://codex.wordpress.org/Using_Permalinks

Extend (Plugins Directory):
http://wordpress.org/extend

Other Resources

These links and applications and plug-ins may not have been developed by WordPress, but they can greatly enhance your blogging experience.

Blog editors

Bleezer:
http://alchemii.net/bleezer/

Blogo:
http://drinkbrainjuice.com/blogo

MarsEdit:
http://red-sweater.com/marsedit/

ScribeFire:
http://scribefire.com/

Windows Live Writer:
http://windowslivewriter.spaces.live.com/

Browsers

Firefox:
http://getfirefox.com

Opera:
www.opera.com

Color schemes

Colour Lovers:
www.colourlovers.com

Kuler:
http://kuler.adobe.com

Creative Commons

Creative Commons:
http://creativecommons.org

CSS and design

A List Apart:
http://alistapart.com

CSS Zen Garden:
http://csszengarden.com

OTHER RESOURCES

Favicons

Favikon:
http://favikon.com

Google AdSense

Google AdSense:
www.google.com/adsense

MySQL

MySQL & MySQL Administrator:
http://mysql.com

OPML

Outline Processor Markup Language (OPML):
http://opml.org

PHP

PHP:
http://php.net

WordPress plug-ins

All In One SEO Pack:
http://wordpress.org/extend/plugins/
all-in-one-seo-pack/

Google XML Sitemaps:
http://wordpress.org/extend/plugins/
google-sitemap-generator/

Contact Form 7:
http://wordpress.org/extend/plugins/
contact-form-7/

Google Analytics for WordPress:
http://wordpress.org/extend/plugins/
google-analytics-for-wordpress/

Add To Any:
http://wordpress.org/extend/plugins/
add-to-any/

Google Analyticator:
http://wordpress.org/extend/plugins/
google-analyticator/

NextGEN Gallery:
http://wordpress.org/extend/plugins/
nextgen-gallery/

GD Star Rating:
http://wordpress.org/extend/plugins/
gd-star-rating/

WP Super Cache:
http://wordpress.org/extend/plugins/
wp-super-cache/

Sociable:
http://wordpress.org/extend/plugins/
sociable/

Twitter Tools:
http://wordpress.org/extend/plugins/
twitter-tools/

Easy AdSense:
http://wordpress.org/extend/plugins/
easy-adsenser/

Yet Another Related Posts Plugin (YARP):
http://wordpress.org/extend/plugins/
yet-another-related-posts-plugin/

Podcatchers

iTunes:
www.apple.com/itunes

Zune:
http://social.zune.net/podcasts

Juice:
http://juicereceiver.sourceforge.net

Winamp:
www.winamp.com

RSS readers

Google Reader:
http://reader.google.com

NetNewsWire:
www.newsgator.com/individuals/
netnewswire/

OTHER RESOURCES

Typography

Typetester:
www.typetester.org

Validators

W3C Validators:
http://validator.w3.org

INDEX

INDEX